PENGUIN BOOKS

THE READER'S QUOTATION BOOK

Steven Gilbar edited *The Book Book*; *Good Books: A Book Lover's Companion*; and *The Open Door: When Writers First Learned to Read*. When he is not reading, he is a lawyer, living with his wife and son in Santa Barbara.

Doris Grumbach is the author of *Chamber Music*, *The Ladies*, and other books. Her memoir *Coming into the End Zone* is soon to be published. She lives in Sargentville, Maine.

THE
READER'S
QUOTATION
BOOK

A LITERARY COMPANION

EDITED BY
STEVEN GILBAR

PENGUIN BOOKS

PENGUIN BOOKS
Published by the Penguin Group
Viking Penguin, a division of Penguin Books USA Inc.,
375 Hudson Street, New York, New York 10014, U.S.A.
Penguin Books Ltd, 27 Wrights Lane,
London W8 5TZ, England
Penguin Books Australia Ltd, Ringwood,
Victoria, Australia
Penguin Books Canada Ltd, 10 Alcorn Avenue, Suite 300,
Toronto, Ontario, Canada M4V 3B2
Penguin Books (N.Z.) Ltd, 182–190 Wairau Road,
Auckland 10, New Zealand

Penguin Books Ltd, Registered Offices:
Harmondsworth, Middlesex, England

First published in the United States of America
by The Pushcart Press 1990
Published in Penguin Books 1991

3 5 7 9 10 8 6 4 2

LIBRARY OF CONGRESS CATALOGING IN PUBLICATION DATA
The Reader's quotation book: a literary companion/edited by Steven
Gilbar.
p.   cm.
Reprint. Originally published: Pushcart Press, 1990.
ISBN 0 14 01.5839 1
1. Books and reading—Quotations, maxims, etc.   I. Gilbar,
Steven.
Z1003.R27   1991
808.88′2—dc20   91–16619

Printed in the United States of America

CONTENTS

INTRODUCTION
by Doris Grumbach

At three and a half I learned to read. At seven, I was seized by the strange idea that one was required to read a book a day. I've done that, willy-nilly, ever since. I have no memory of my first French meal, my first taste of fresh asparagus, or my first swim in the ocean, but I recall with great clarity the first book I loved. It was a terrible novel (I now know) by William J. Locke and it was called *Stella Maris*. I remember with equal brightness the glory of the day I was first allowed to use the upstairs, adult floor of the St. Amsterdam branch of the New York Public Library. J. D. Salinger, I learned later, used the same library at about the same time. Unfortunately we never met in those blessed rooms. These are my only qualifications for writing this introduction: a reader almost from birth, the quantity of volumes I have absorbed, the lifelong passion I bring to the act.

A few years ago it became the habit of my partner in Wayward Books, a bookstore we had in Washington D.C., and her manager, to write on an A-frame blackboard in front of the store just such quotations as are contained in this volume. They changed it daily.

Many people stopped to read them; some copied them down on their way to work, on slips of paper they dropped into their briefcases. Others told us they walked a block out of their way to read the day's aphorism. One of our perennial favorites was by Erasmus: "When I get a little money I buy books; and if any is left, I buy food and clothes."

This pleasant activity ended abruptly when the city gave the store a ticket for $500. It seems we were obstructing city property. Faithful customers signed a petition to have the blackboard restored, a petition that was denied. But it did convince the judge to lower the fine considerably. Quotations, it appeared, were some sort of danger, seditious in nature, and likely to fall on you violently if you stood near them.

I have now reached an age when reading as a life-support system has turned into re-reading, for the same purpose. Cynthia Ozick's comment in this volume reflects my conviction that "There's a paradox in rereading. You read the first time for rediscovery: an encounter with the confirming emotions. But you reread for discovery: you go to the known to figure out the workings of the unknown, the why of the familiar how." Nabokov agreed: "All great reading is rereading," he wrote, knowing as Cynthia Ozick and I and many others do, that returning to remembered pleasure and finding it still pleasurable is one of a devoted old reader's greatest pleasures.

I read these quotations about readers and reading, savoring every one. Ever since I learned from Franz

Kafka that "a book is an axe to the frozen sea around us" I've been on the lookout for other sharp, pointed remarks like these, and here they are, gathered under one roof, to browse through, to quote in speeches or display at dinner parties, or just enjoy, one by one, like olives, at odd moments in the day or night.

In another way, as a writer, I know that Mallarmé was right when he said that "the world exists to be put in a book." Writers are grateful if they can squeeze even a jagged little piece of the world into their texts, a narrow corner of what they know about it onto their pages. And the reader is grateful to be able to recognize it or better, to extend his own restricted existence into a thousand others he discovers through a book. He finds he can escape the tedium of his days by entering another world that is the writer's. One of the sentences I admire in the book you are holding is by Gustave Flaubert: "The one way of tolerating existence is to lose oneself in literature as in a perpetual orgy."

It is regarded as *gauche* to drink good brandy down in one gulp, like a shot. Similarly the contents of this book. My advice to you is to sip them slowly, turning these good sentences around in your head the way brandy lovers swish their B. & B. in their large snifters, savoring the bouquet of these literate and aphoristic remarks. Then, as is my wont, reread them. The process may not be a perpetual orgy, but it will resemble a satisfying cocktail hour.

THE READER'S QUOTATION BOOK

THE GLORY OF READING

Prefer knowledge to wealth, for the one is transitory, the other perpetual.

SOCRATES

I find my joy and solace in literature. There is no gladness that this cannot increase; no sorrow that it cannot lessen. Troubled as I am by the ill health of my wife, by the dangerous condition—sometimes, alas! by death—of my friends, I fly to my studies as the one alleviation of my fears. They do me this service—they make me understand my troubles better, and bear them more patiently.

PLINY

Books delight us when prosperity smiles upon us; they comfort us inseparably when stormy fortune frowns on us.

RICHARD DE BURY

Blessed be God, that hath set up so many clear lamps in His Church! Now, none but the wilfully blind can plead darkness. And blessed be the memory of those His faithful servants that have left their blood, their spirits, their lives, in these precious books; and have willingly wasted themselves into these during monuments, to give light unto others.

JOSEPH HALL

Reading maketh a full man.

FRANCIS BACON

Remember
First to possess his books; for without them
He's but a sot, as I am.
WILLIAM SHAKESPEARE (*The Tempest*)

Books are as lively, and as vigorously productive, as those fabulous dragon's teeth: and being sown up and down, may chance to spring up armed men.
JOHN MILTON

Books are not only titles on their author's monuments, but epitaphs, preserving their memories, be they good, or bad, beyond short lived pyramids, or mausoleum piles of stone.
RICHARD WHITLOCK

No entertainment is so cheap as reading, nor any pleasure so lasting. She will not want new fashions, nor expensive diversions, or variety of company, if she can be amused with an author. . . .
LADY MARY WORTLEY MONTAGU

The use of letters is the principal circumstance that distinguishes a civilized people from a herd of savages incapable of knowledge and reflections.
EDWARD GIBBON

The only end of writing is to enable readers better to enjoy life or better to endure it.
SAMUEL JOHNSON

Books never annoy; they cost little, and they are always at hand, and ready at your call.

WILLIAM COBBETT

> Books are yours,
> Within whose silent chambers treasure lies
> Preserved from age to age; more precious far
> Than that accumulated store of gold
> And orient gems which, for a day of need,
> The sultan hides deep in ancestral tombs,
> These hoards of truth you can unlock at will

WILLIAM WORDSWORTH

The writings of the wise are the only riches our posterity cannot squander.

WALTER SAVAGE LANDOR

It is with books as with men, a very small number play a great part: the rest are confounded with the multitude.

VOLTAIRE

In a well-written book we are presented with the maturest reflections, or the happiest flights, of a mind of uncommon excellence. It is impossible that we can be much accustomed to such companions, without attaining some resemblance of them. When I read Thomson, I become Thomson; when I read Milton, I become Milton. I find myself a sort of intellectual chameleon, assuming the color of the substance on which I rest.

WILLIAM GODWIN

[Books] are the nearest to our thoughts: they wind into the heart; the poet's verse slides into the current of our blood. We read them when young, we remember them when old. We read there of what has happened to others; we feel that it has happened to ourselves. They are to be had everywhere cheap and good. We breathe but the air of books; we owe everything to their authors, on this side of barbarism; and we pay them easily with contempt, while living, and with an epitaph, when dead!

WILLIAM HAZLITT

Wise books,
   For half the truth they hold are
      honored tombs.

GEORGE ELIOT

For books are more than books, they are the life
The very heart and core of ages past
The reason why men lived and worked and died
The essence and quintessence of their lives.

AMY LOWELL

Reading in general is one of my methods of recuperation; consequently it is a part of that which enables me to escape from myself, to wander in strange sciences and strange souls. . . .

FRIEDRICH NIETZCHE

It is not all books that are as dull as their readers. There are probably words addressed to our condition exactly, which, if we would really hear and understand, would be more salutary than the morning or the spring to our lives, and possibly put a new aspect on the face of things for us. How many a man has dated a new era in his life from the reading of a book. The book exists for us, perchance, which will explain our miracles and reveal new ones.

HENRY DAVID THOREAU

The one way of tolerating existence is to lose oneself in literature as in a perpetual orgy.

GUSTAVE FLAUBERT

What power in books!
They mingle gloom and splendour, as I've oft,
In thunderous sunsets, seen the thunder-piles
Seamed with dull fire and fiercest glory-rents.
They awe me to my knees, as if I stood in presence of
a king.

ALEXANDER SMITH

Think what a book is. It is a portion of the eternal
mind caught in its process through the world,
stamped in an instant, and preserved for eternity.

LORD HOUGHTON

There are books which take rank in our life with parents and lovers and passionate experiences, so medic-
inal, so stringent, so revolutionary, so authoritative.

RALPH WALDO EMERSON

The world exists to be put in a book.

STÉPHANE MALLARMÉ

Each [book] is a mummified soul embalmed in cere-
cloth and natron of leather and printer's ink. Each
cover of a true book enfolds the concentrated essence
of a man. The personalities of the writers have folded
into the thinnest shadows, as their bodies into impal-
pable dust, yet here are their very spirits at your command.

SIR ARTHUR CONAN DOYLE

Every reader who holds a book in his hand is free of the inmost minds of men past and present; their lives both within and without the pale of their uttered thoughts are unveiled to him; he needs no introduction to the greatest.

FREDERIC HARRISON

Of all the inanimate objects, of all of man's creations, books are the nearest to us, for they contain our very thought, our ambitions, our indignations, our illusions, our fidelity to truth, and our persistent leaning towards error. But most of all they resemble us in their precarious hold on life.

JOSEPH CONRAD

Reading you grow more gentle, pensive grave;
They teach you as the dawn lights up a cloister,
And as their warm beams penetrate your heart
You are appeased and thrill with stronger life.

VICTOR HUGO (from *L'Année Terrible*)

It is a man's duty to have books. A library is not a luxury, but one of the necessities of life.

HENRY WARD BEECHER

If we could buy knowledge, prudence, forethought and all the elementary virtues out of sevenpenny editions of standard authors, we should long ago have become a race of unbearably perfect archangels. And we are still quite a little lower than the angels. None the less, it is possible that our reading, if so be we read wisely, may save us to a certain extent from some of the serious forms of trouble; or if we get into trouble, as we most certainly shall, may teach us how to come out of it decently.

RUDYARD KIPLING

When others fail him, the wise man looks
To the sure companionship of books.

ANDREW LANG

Without the word, without the writing of books, there is no history, there is no concept of humanity. And if anyone wants to try to enclose in a small space, in a single house or a single room, the history of the human spirit and to make it his own, he can only do this in the form of a collection of books.

HERMANN HESSE

Books are man's rational protests against the irratio-
nal, man's pitiful protest against the implacable,
man's ideal against the world's real, man's word
against the cosmic dumbness, man's life against the
planetary death, man's repartee to the God without
him. Whoever touches a book touches not only "a
man" but Man. Man is the animal who weeps and
laughs—*and writes*. If the first Prometheus brought
fire from heaven in a fennel-stalk, the last will take it
back—*in a book*.

JOHN COWPER POWYS

Eyes that never read, remain blind to the phantom
dead and to the unseen presences that walk the
earth—cannot call up the past world to redress the
troubled balance of the present—cannot move, like
Persephone, both amid the fleeting beauty of the living spring and among the ghostly meadows of eternal
asphodel.

F. L. LUCAS

We live in a cultural continuum in which we are free
to move back and forth through the centuries. Books
are islands in the ocean of time. They are also oases
in the deserts of Time.

LAWRENCE CLARK POWELL

No foreign travel is so consistently exciting, rewarding, as travels in a mind. And it is the unique quality of the great writers that they throw their minds, their souls wide open to our exploration. They cannot help doing so. It is by revelation that they live; they are obsessed with the understanding of people and the world; and all the people are themselves, the world is their own world.

JOYCE CARY

The world of books is the most remarkable creation of man. Nothing else that he builds ever lasts. Monuments fall, nations perish, civilizations grow old and die out; and, after an era of darkness, new races build others. But in the world of books are volumes that have seen this happen again and again, and yet live on, still young, still as fresh as the day they were written, still telling men's hearts of the hearts of men centuries dead.

CLARENCE DAY

The aim of literary study is not to amuse the hours of leisure; it is to awake oneself, it is to be alive, to intensify one's capacity for pleasure, for sympathy, and for comprehension. It is not to affect one hour, but twenty-four hours. It is to change utterly one's relations with the world.

ARNOLD BENNETT

Real reading cannot be pure recreation. . . . The writer's business is to lay you flat if he can, to make you feel the active presence of forces and influences, to rouse, startle, interest, amuse, satisfy.

ARTHUR CHRISTOPHER BENSON

And books! those miraculous memories of high thoughts and golden moods; those silver shells, tremulous with the wonderful secrets of the ocean of life; those love-letters that pass from hand to hand of a thousand lovers that never meet. . . .

RICHARD LE GALLIENNE

Books contain the thoughts and dreams of men, their hopes and strivings and all their immortal parts. It's in books that most of us learn how splendidly worth while life is. . . .

CHRISTOPHER MORLEY

I cannot imagine life without literature, without books. The fate of the human being is to be born mortal with a knowledge of eternity. Lost in such a void of time, our own measured years are not long. But because we have literature, art, and music, our great past can become the present. We can span the gaps of generations and establish an intimate relationship with someone dead for hundreds of years. The life of the human being is a lonely life, but the lives of those who have denied themselves a knowledge of our common culture are doubly lonely.

ERIK CHRISTIAN HAUGAARD

The world may be kind or unkind, it may seem to us to be hastening on the wings of enlightenment and progress to an imminent millennium, or it may weigh us down with the sense of insoluble difficulty and irremediable wrong; but whatever else it be, so long as we have good health and a good library, it can hardly be dull.

EARL OF BALFOUR

Books offer an escape, but it is an escape *into* something larger, not *from* something larger; it is an escape into hazard, not from hazard. A dictator escapes not by fleeing into a library, but by a midnight flight to the Dominican Republic.

HARRY GOLDEN

It is the writer's privilege to help man endure by lifting his heart, by reminding him of the courage and honor and hope and pride and compassion and pity and sacrifice which have been the glory of his past. The poet's voice need not merely be the record of man, it can be one of the props, the pillars to help him endure and prevail.

WILLIAM FAULKNER

Reading is a privileged pleasure because each of us enjoys it, quite complexly, in ways not replicable by anyone else. But there is enough structural common ground in the text itself so that we can talk to each other, even sometimes persuade each other, about what we read: and that many-voiced conversation, with which, thankfully, we shall never have done, is one of the most gratifying responses to literary creation, second only to reading itself.

ROBERT ALTER

People seldom read a book which is given to them.

SAMUEL JOHNSON

One can be amused or excited by a book that one's intellect simply refused to take seriously.

GEORGE ORWELL

A book—a well-composed book—is a magic carpet on which we are wafted to a world that we cannot enter in any other way. Yet, in another sense, all true works of fiction have their scenes laid in the same country, and the events take place in the same climate: that country, that climate which we all long for and in our several ways strive to reach—the region where truth is eternal and man immortal and flowers never fade.

CAROLINE GORDON

[A novel is a] work in which the greatest powers of the mind are displayed; in which the most thorough knowledge of human nature, the happiest delineation of its varieties, the liveliest effusions of wit or humor, are conveyed to the world in the best chosen language.

JANE AUSTEN (*Northanger Abbey*)

Fiction is art and art is the triumph over chaos . . . to celebrate a world that lies spread out around us like a bewildering and stupendous dream.

JOHN CHEEVER

We need myths to get by. We need story; otherwise the tremendous randomness of experience overwhelms us. Story is what penetrates.

ROBERT COOVER

Reading is the sole means by which we slip, involuntarily, often helplessly, into another's skin, another's voice, another's soul.

JOYCE CAROL OATES

[S]he had but a single weapon against the world of crudity surrounding her; the books she took out of the municipal library, and above all, the novels. . . . They . . . offered the possibility of an imaginary escape from a life she found unsatisfying.

MILAN KUNDERA (*The Unbearable Lightness of Being*)

The greatest thing to be gained from the reading of books is the desire to truly communicate with one's fellow man. To read a book properly is to wake up and live, to acquire a renewed interest in one's neighbors, more especially those who are alien to us in every way.

HENRY MILLER

[G]reat fiction can change our lives; turn us around corners. No movie ever did that to me. I might walk and talk a bit differently for a few minutes after leaving an effective film but that's about it. Novels have heft; films are filmy.

JOHN BARTH

In its complicated, possibly even mysterious way, the novel is an instrument for delving into the human truth.

SAUL BELLOW

A great novelist must open the reader's heart, allow the reader to remember the vastness and glory—and shame and shabbiness—of what it is to be human.

CAROLYN SEE

[Reading novels] is a way of saying who I am, a way of finding out what world I live in. I don't read magazines, don't go to the movies, but if someone says 'Here is this novel,' I read it more times than not, as an act of profit and delight, as a battered act of faith.

ROGER SALE

[T]he invented characters of fiction, like recorded music, come to life through some element which we ourselves supply. It is we, the readers, who give these imaginary creatures a setting in time and space somewhere within ourselves, which enables them to move freely and suddenly, to impose their destinies.

FRANÇOIS MAURIAC

There are always those things in the *Times* every year and a half that say 'Is the novel dead?' And I think about what Dr. Johnson said about London: 'When a man is tired of London, he is tired of life.' Well, the reader who is tired of the novel is ready for suicide.

ALLEN GURGANUS

Without a basic living experience we understand nothing, not even diaries and novels. But the novels can enormously extend and enrich that basic experience; as a great house can enlarge the appreciation of a village carpenter.

JOYCE CARY

If fiction is to help at all in the process of living, it is by illuminating its conflicts and its ambiguities. We read to find out more about what it is like to be a human being, not to be told how to be one.

PENELOPE LIVELY

Novels are for understanding and finding out about people; language is for making things plain; the more a novelist thinks it is important for the reader to understand exactly what he means, the more trouble he must take to express himself as simply as he can contrive. This is so much more difficult than most people—including some writers, think, that interesting simplicity is at a premium.

ELIZABETH JANE HOWARD

The novel is something that never was before and will not be again.

EUDORA WELTY

In fiction, truth is the search for truth, nothing is pre-established and knowledge is only what both of us — reader and writer—can imagine.

CARLOS FUENTES

Popular novels in our age might serve the same function as stained-glass windows did in the Middle Ages.

ANDREW GREELEY

Today there are a lot of novelists who seem to be writing to be reviewed, not read.

PETE HAMILL

It is no accident that books are sacred to civilization. They open the past to us. A book is magical; it transcends time and space.

DANIEL J. BOORSTIN

Great works of imaginative literature . . .
are hospitals where we heal . . .
when they are evil works they are
battlefields where we get injured.
     TED HUGHES

[B]ooks are wonderful things: to sit alone in a room
and laugh and cry, because you are reading, and still
be safe when you close the book; and having finished
it, discover you are changed, yet unchanged! To be
able to visit the City of Invention at will, depart at
will—that is all, really, education is about.
     FAY WELDON

Literature is inescapably political. . . . It is in the act
of reading that we define our notions about the
world, what we judge to be right or wrong, important or unimportant, acceptable or unacceptable; literature is the testing ground of the imagination,
where we decide who we are and what sort of society
we live in or should be living in. You tell me your
favorite novelists and I'll tell you whom you vote for,
or whether you vote at all.
     STEPHEN VIZINCZEY

[T]he line between experience and reading often becomes blurry. Reading is experience. A biography of
any literary person ought to deal at length and in detail with what he read and when, for in some sense,
we are what we read.
     JOSEPH EPSTEIN

Reading a book is only the beginning, the first step in the relationship. After you've finished it, the book enters on its real career. It stands there as a badge, a blackmailer, a monument, a scar. It's both a flaw in the room, like a crack in the plaster, and a decoration. The contents of someone's bookcase are part of his history, like an ancestral portrait.

ANATOLE BROYARD

A sense of reality, of showing great people as they really were, is one of the best things about biography.

MARCHETTE CHUTE

[B]iographies of the great are silent about the bad books they read and liked as they are silent about the good books they were made to read and did not like.

HAROLD NICOLSON

I have always suspected that authors lie about the books they read, their purported influences, much as men lie about their sex lives; they are at once ashamed and vain, reluctant to be judged, hiding behind a safe parapet of Joyce and Proust and Kafka.

BRIAN GLANVILLE

My life has been greatly influenced by many books which I have never read.

ASHLEIGH BRILLIANT

If Queen Elizabeth or Frederick the Great or Ernest Hemingway were to read their biographies, they would exclaim, 'Ah, my secret is still safe.' But if Natasha Rostov were to read *War and Peace* she would cry out as she covered her face with her hands: 'How did he know, how did he know?'

THORNTON WILDER

[E]nduring fiction, while of its own time, survives the emotional and social conditions of its creation. Non-fiction may be more important to contemporary understanding of the past, present or future, but it is temporal, always subject to revision.

WILLIAM ROBERTSON

As a former English major, I am a sitting duck for Gift Books, and in the past few years I've gotten Dickens, Thackeray, Smollett, Richardson, Emerson, Keats, Boswell and the Brontës, all of them Great, none of them ever read by me, all of them now on my shelf, looking at me and making me feel guilty.

GARRISON KEILLOR

The books we think we ought to read are poky, dull and dry;
The books that we should like to read we are ashamed to buy;
The books that people talk about we never can recall;
And the books that people give us, oh, they're the worst of all.

CAROLYN WELLS (from *On Books*)

Personality is partially an extension of the personal bibliography that every mature adult carries within. The books which we have read provide the most challenging windows into the precious privacy that remains as a steady and sustaining quiet, a centering identity, within all of us.

KEVIN STARR

Books precede and outlast us. They are cemeteries of the living. The solemn buckram sepulchers contain the wildest of life, and the carousing corpses within—begot by an author, realized by a printer, first freed by a paperknife—now wait only for sight to fall on their pages for them to rise up and live—little resurrections performed for every new reader.

PAUL THEROUX

The great gift is the passion for reading. It is cheap, it consoles, it distracts, it excites. It gives you knowledge of the world and experience of a wide kind. It is a moral illumination.

ELIZABETH HARDWICK

Why are we reading, if not in hope that the writer will magnify and dramatize our days, will illuminate and inspire us with wisdom, courage and the hope of meaningfulness, and press upon our minds the deepest mysteries, so we may feel again their majesty and power?

ANNIE DILLARD

Many a book is like a key to unknown chambers within the castle of one's own self.

FRANZ KAFKA

People who don't read are brutes.

EUGENE IONESCO

I like being around books. It makes me feel civilized. The only way to do all the things you'd like to do is to read.

TOM CLANCY

. . . . The ones of little reading
Or who never read for love, are many places.
They are in the house of power, and many houses . . .

ROBERT PINSKY

I have often wondered how anyone who does not read, by which I mean daily, having some book going all the time, can make it through life . . . Indeed if I were required to make a sharp division in the very nature of people, I would be tempted to make it there: readers and nonreaders of books.

WILLIAM BRINKLEY (from *The Lost Ship*)

Civilized man is a reader. Irrevocably he would appear to be committed to the scanning of small black marks on plane surfaces. It is, when you come to think it over, an odd gesture, like the movement the camera catches of the heads of a tennis audience. But there it is—we are readers, and it's too late to change.

CLIFTON FADIMAN

Once in a very rare year, there comes along a new book, and I say, as I'm reading, as my eyes eat words without a blink, as my heart and mind grab each other, This, I say, is The Best Book. I know before the first page is gone. I sense it building. And as the book finishes, I go as slow as I can. I don't want to leave this book's world. . . .

JILL ROBINSON

Many readers look continually for the work of genius or at least of brilliance, deep compassion and understanding. . . . [P]erhaps it would be wiser to enjoy sane balance, quirky invention, shrewd observations, a touch of wit; in other words, we should be satisfied with competent professional skill while we wait for the occasional new masterpiece to shamble along.

HERBERT GOLD

Through engagement with others, literature lets us imagine what it would be like to be different.

DENIS DONOGHUE

[I]n reading ... stories, you can be many different people in many different places, doing things you would never have a chance to do in ordinary life. It's amazing that those twenty-six little marks of the alphabet can arrange themselves on the pages of a book and accomplish all that. Readers are lucky— they will never be bored or lonely.

NATALIE BABBITT

Reading means ... to be ready to catch a voice that makes itself heard when you least expect it, a voice that comes from an unknown source, from some where beyond the book, beyond the author, beyond the convention of writing: from the unsaid, from what the world has not yet said of itself and does not yet have the words to say.

ITALO CALVINO

In all this willful world
of thud and thump and thunder
man's relevance to books
continues to declare.

Books are meat and medicine
and flame and flight and flower
steel, stitch, cloud and clout,
and drumbeats on the air.

GWENDOLYN BROOKS (from *Books Feed and Cure and Chortle and Collide*)

You are an invited guest on a literary journey. You think your load is light—the weight of a hardcover or paperback book. But like Saint Christopher's burden—which he took without thinking and which grew heavier with each step through the water—a well-crafted book holds similar weight.

JILL PATON WALSH

Without these skills [of reading and writing], we are prisoners of our own limitations, sentenced to exist on scraps from life's banquet.

JOANNA BARNES

With a good book one can always enjoy, tête-à-tête, the mind of a man that one likes and respects. And indeed few authors are, in my experience, as good in the flesh as in print.

F. L. LUCAS

HOW TO READ

Some books are to be tasted, others to be swallowed, and some few to be chewed and digested: that is, some books are to be read only in parts; others to be read, but not curiously; and some few to be read wholly, and with diligence and attention.

FRANCIS BACON

who reads

Incessantly, and to his reading brings not
A spirit and judgment equal or superior,
(And what he brings, what needs he elsewhere seek?)
Uncertain and unsettl'd still remains,
Deep verst in books and shallow in himself,
Crude or intoxicate, collecting toys,
And trifles for choice matters, worth a spunge;
As children gathering pebbles on the shore.

JOHN MILTON

Reading furnishes the mind only with materials of knowledge; it is thinking makes what we read ours. We are of the ruminating kind, and it is not enough to cram ourselves with a great load of collections; unless we chew them over again, they will not give us strength and nourishment.

JOHN LOCKE

To take measures wholly from books, without looking into men and business, is like travelling in a map, where though countries and cites are well enough distinguished, yet villages and private seats are either overlooked, or too generally marked for a stranger to find; therefore he that would be a master must draw from the life, as well as copy from originals, and join theory and experience together.

JEREMY COLLIER

Bookful blockhead, ignorantly read,
With loads of learned lumber in his head.

ALEXANDER POPE

A reader finds little in a book save what he puts there.
But in a great book he finds space to put many things.

JOSEPH JOUBERT

Lay down a method also for your reading; let it be in a consistent and consecutive course, and not in that desultory and unmethodical manner, in which many people read scraps of different authors, upon different subjects.

EARL OF CHESTERFIELD

Let us read with method, and propose to ourselves
an end to which all our studies may point. Through
neglect of this rule, gross ignorance disgraces great
readers, who, by skipping hastily and irregularly from
one subject to another, render themselves incapable of
combining their ideas.

EDWARD GIBBON

There are only four kinds of readers.
  The first is like the hour-glass; their
reading being as the sand, it runs in
and runs out, and leaves no vestige behind.
  The second is like the sponge, which
imbibes everything, and returns it in nearly
the same state, only a little dirtier.
  A third is like a jelly-bag, allowing all
that is pure to pass away, retaining only
the refuse and dregs.
  And the fourth is like the slaves in the
diamond mines, who, casting aside all that
is worthless, retain only pure gems.

SAMUEL TAYLOR COLERIDGE

Books are a world in themselves, it is true; but they
are not the only world. The world itself is a volume
larger than all the libraries in it.

WILLIAM HAZLITT

The profit of books is according to the sensibility of the reader. The profoundest thought or passion sleeps as in a mine, until an equal mind finds and publishes it.

RALPH WALDO EMERSON

Every reader finds himself. The writer's work is merely a kind of optical instrument that makes it possible for the reader to discern what, without this book, he would perhaps never have seen in himself.

MARCEL PROUST

In a way we only learn from books we understand; the author of a book we do not understand would have to learn from us.

J. W. VON GOETHE

To read a book in the true sense, to read it, that is, not as a critic but in the spirit of enjoyment—is to lay aside for the moment one's own personality and to become a part of the author.

LESLIE STEPHEN

                              We get no good
By being ungenerous even to a book,
And calculating profits—so much help
By so much reading. It is rather when
We gloriously forget ourselves and plunge
Soul-forward, headlong, into a book's profound,
Impassioned for its beauty and salt of truth—
'Tis then we get the right good from a book.

ELIZABETH BARRETT BROWNING

Thoughtless, absent reading is very much like walking blindfold through beautiful country. We should read, not in order to forget ourselves and our daily lives, but on the contrary, in order to gain a firmer, more conscious, more mature grip on our own lives. We should come to a book not as a frightened schoolboy to a forbidding teacher or as the town drunkard to a schnapps bottle, but as a mountain climber to the Alps or a soldier to an arsenal, not as fugitives from life.

HERMANN HESSE

Very few literate persons are able to read . . . that is, to carry away from a piece of printed matter anything like a correct idea of its contents. They are more or less adept at passing printed matter through their mind, after a fashion, . . . but this is not reading. Reading implies a use of the reflective faculty, and very few have that faculty developed much beyond the anthropoid stage, let alone possessing it at a stage of development which makes reading practicable.

ALBERT JAY NOCK

A good reader is one who has imagination, memory, a dictionary, and some artistic sense.

VLADIMIR NABOKOV

When you think of being a good reader, you tend to think of yourself or somebody as having a sharp eye, quick intelligence who pays attention, follows this resonance or meaning or that, and has a good memory for what happened before and all that admirable true crap. But who thinks of the reader as an oral interpreter? When I read a traditional novel I never remember anything except language, the rhythms in the language patterns, and I do have a good memory for that. I think I forgot the basic plot of *Middlemarch* hours after I read it, and it was of course a terrific book. But the impression, the quality of its style—that I think I shall remember forever.

WILLIAM GASS

To read well, that is to read true books in a true spirit, is a noble exercise, and one that will task the reader more than any exercise which the customs of the day esteem. It requires a training such as the athletes underwent, the steady intention almost of the whole life to this object.

HENRY DAVID THOREAU

The process of reading is not a half-sleep, but in highest sense, an exercise, a gymnast's struggle; that the reader is to do something for himself, must be on the alert, must himself or herself construct indeed the poem, argument, history, metaphysical essay—the text furnishing the hints, the clue, the start or framework.

WALT WHITMAN

If any one finds that he never reads serious literature, if all his reading is frothy and trashy, he would do well to try to train himself to like books that the general agreement of cultivated and sound-thinking persons has placed among the classics. It is as discreditable to the mind to be unfit for sustained mental effort as it is to the body of a young man to be unfit for sustained physical effort.

THEODORE ROOSEVELT

[T]he intuitive sensations of delight or illumination or their absences that accompany a purely gratuitous, spontaneous reading of a book.... One scans the pages as one scans life, half asleep in the dream of sequentiality, now and then poked awake by a flash of beauty, or the crackle of truth.

JOHN UPDIKE

There is no way of reading as one runs . . . when we come to the examination of any highly developed art.

LOUISE BOGAN

Read properly, fewer books than a hundred would suffice for a liberal education. Read superficially, the British Museum Library might still leave the student a barbarian.

A. R. ORAGE

It is an error to think that vast reading will automatically produce any such knowledge or understanding. Neither Chaucer with his forty books, nor Shakespeare with perhaps half a dozen, in folio, can be considered illiterate. A man can learn more music by working on a Bach fugue until he can take it apart and put it together, than by playing through ten dozen heterogeneous albums.

EZRA POUND

In the past hundred years almost all English men and women have been taught—but never have they been taught *what*—to read and write. Reading has been offered to them as a drug to soothe their nerves and fill their brief leisure and has also been presented to them as something easy, like eating, swimming or "kicking a ball about." Seldom has it been revealed to them as an art, though in truth the reader should be as carefully and patiently trained as the writer.

OSBERT SITWELL

In anything fit to be called by the name of reading, the process itself should be absorbing and voluptuous; we should gloat over a book, be rapt clean out of ourselves.

ROBERT LOUIS STEVENSON

No book, any more than helpful words, can do anything decisive if the person concerned is not already prepared through quite invisible influences for a deeper receptivity and absorption, if his hour of self-communion has not come anyway.

RAINER MARIA RILKE

The adult relation to books is one of absorbing rather than being absorbed.

ANTHONY BURGESS

One only reads well that which one reads with some quite personal purpose. It may be to acquire some power. It can be out of hatred for the author.

PAUL VALÉRY

There is only one situation I can think of in which men and women make an effort to read better than they usually do. When they are in love and reading a love letter, they read for all they are worth. They read every word three ways; they read between the lines and in the margins . . . They may even take the punctuation into account. Then, if never before or after, they read.

MORTIMER J. ADLER

If the book we are reading does not wake us, as with a fist hammering on our skull, why then do we read it? So that it shall make us happy? Good God, we would also be happy if we had no books, and such books as make us happy we could, if need be, write ourselves. But what we must have are those books which come upon us like ill-fortune, and distress us deeply, like the death of one we love better than ourselves, like suicide. . . .

FRANZ KAFKA

To read great literature as if it did not have upon us an urgent design . . . is to do little more than to make entries in a librarian's catalogue.

GEORGE STEINER

To read a book, in my own case, is always a sort of combat, in which I ask myself whether the author is going to overcome me, and persuade me, and convince me, or even vex me.

ARTHUR CHRISTOPHER BENSON

The gift of creative reading, like all natural gifts, must be nourished or it will atrophy. And you nourish it, in much the same way you nourish the gift of writing— you read, think, talk, look, listen, hate, fear, love, weep—and bring all of your life like a sieve to what you read. That which is not worthy of your gift will quickly pass through, but the gold remains.

KATHARINE PATERSON

As you read [a book] word by word and page by page, you participate in its creation, just as a cellist playing a Bach suite participates, note by note, in the creation, the coming-to-be, the existence, of the music. And, as you read and re-read, the book of course participates in the creation of *you*, your thoughts and feelings, the size and temper of your soul.

URSULA K. LEGUIN

The process of reading is reciprocal: the book is no more than a formula, to be furnished out with images out of the reader's mind.

ELIZABETH BOWEN

There are certain chemicals will remain quiescent if they are mixed with one set of substances, but if they are mixed with another set they rise and foam and vapour, so a book requires to be mixed with something in the soul of the reader, before there is any motion or energy put forth.

ARTHUR CHRISTOPHER BENSON

To read for the mere luxury of reading is to miss the best things which they have to give. In every true companionship there is an interchange; one gives as well as receives. The best reading—the most intelligent and fruitful—involves a community of interest and thought between the reader and the writer.

HAMILTON WRIGHT MABIE

What can we see, read, acquire, but ourselves. Take the book, my friend, and read your eyes out, you will never find there what I find.

RALPH WALDO EMERSON

In reality every reader is, while he is reading, the reader of his own self.

MARCEL PROUST

The novelist in America today benefits ... from a group of readers who, beset with an unprecedented variety of diversions, continue to read with great taste and intelligence.

JOHN CHEEVER

Unless a reader is able to give something of himself, he cannot get from a novel the best it has to give. And if he isn't able to do that, he had better not read it at all. There is no obligation to read a work of fiction.

W. SOMERSET MAUGHAM

Reading is a discontinuous and fragmentary operation ... In the spreading expanse of the writing, the reader's attention isolates some minimal segments, juxtapositions of words, metaphors, syntactic nexuses, logical passages, lexical peculiarities that prove to possess an extremely concentrated density of meaning. They are like elemental particles making up the work's nucleus, around which all the rest revolves. Or else like the void at the bottom of the vortex which sucks in and swallows currents. It is through these apertures that, in barely perceptible flashes, the truth the book may bear is revealed, its ultimate substance.

ITALO CALVINO

A book consists of two layers: on top, the readable layer ... and underneath, a layer that was inaccessible. You only sense its existence in a moment of distraction from the literal reading, the way you see childhood through a child. It would take forever to tell what you see, and it would be pointless.

MARGUERITE DURAS

It was in Grossgmain that I first discovered reading. This was a sudden discovery which proved decisive for my subsequent life. This discovery—that literature can at any moment provide the mathematical solution to life and one's own existence provided that it is put into gear and operated as though it were mathematics, so that in time it becomes a form of higher mathematics and ultimately the supreme mathematical art, which can be called reading only when we have mastered it completely.

THOMAS BERNHARD

It's not macho to read a book? Nonsense. Reading is a stouthearted activity, disporting courage, keenness, stick-to-it-ness. It is also, in my experience, one of the most thrilling and enduring delights of life, equal to a home run, a slam-dunk, or breaking the four-minute mile.

IRVING STONE

One reads at one's own speed, in short snatches on the subway or in long, voluptuous withdrawals from the world. One proceeds through a big, complex novel . . . like an exceptionally well-heeled tourist in a foreign landscape, going slowly or fast depending on the roads, on one's own mood and on the attractions along the way. If one loses something, one can always go back to pick it up.

VINCENT CANBY

The true felicity of a lover of books is the luxurious turning of page by page, the surrender, not meanly abject, but deliberate and cautious, with your wits about you, as you deliver yourself into the keeping of the book. . . . This I call reading.

EDITH WHARTON

Resist all temptation to make an end of a book, seek to conserve your literary experiences; linger over words and phrases, become thrall to a thought, or convert to an idea. Read, in short, as you taste fruit or savor wine, or enjoy friendship, or love, or life.

HOLBROOK JACKSON

Few people have ever truly learned to read. The moral is, read slowly. Take ample time. Pause where the punctuation bids one pause; note each and every comma; wait a moment between a period and the next capital letter. And pause when sense bids you pause, that is, when you have not understood.

LANE COOPER

What I enjoy in a narrative is not directly its content or even the structure, but rather the abrasions I impose upon the surface: I read on, I skip, I look up, I dip in again.

ROLAND BARTHES

Mor liked to tear a book apart as he read it, breaking the back, thumbing and turning down the pages, commenting and underlining. He liked to have his books close to him, upon a table, upon the floor, at least upon open shelves. Seeing them so near and so destroyed, he could feel that they were now almost inside his head.

IRIS MURDOCH (*The Sandcastle*)

Reading is a pleasure of the mind, which means that it is a little like a sport: your eagerness and knowledge and quickness count for something. The fun of reading is not that something is told you, but that you stretch your mind. Your own imagination works along with the author's, or even goes beyond his. Your experience, compared with his, yields the same or different conclusions, and your ideas develop as you understand his.

BENNETT CERF

Reading without subsequent reflection is ridiculous; it is a proof equally of folly and of vanity.

ARNOLD BENNETT

A man cannot turn over anything in his mind unless he knows it; he should, therefore, learn something; but it is only when he has turned it over that he can be said to know it.

ARTHUR SCHOPENHAUER

RE-READING

The reading which has pleased, will please when re-peated ten times.

HORACE

The first time I read an excellent book it is to me just as if I had gained a new friend; when I read over a book I have perused before, it resembles the meeting with an old one.

OLIVER GOLDSMITH

I have no pleasure from books which equals that of reading over for the hundredth time great productions which I almost know by heart.

THOMAS MACAULAY

I almost always take refuge in the same books, few in numbers, books exactly fitting my needs. Perhaps it is not in my nature to read much, or variously: a library makes me ill. Suspicion, even hostility toward new books is nearer to my instincts than 'toleration.'

FRIEDRICH NIETZCHE

No book that will not improve by repeated readings deserves to be read at all.

THOMAS CARLYLE

When I take up a work that I have read before (the oftener the better) I know what I have to expect. The satisfaction is not lessened by being anticipated.

WILLIAM HAZLITT

If one cannot enjoy reading a book over and over again, there is no use in reading at all.

OSCAR WILDE

I would not say that every book worth reading once is worth reading twice over. But I would say that no book of great and established reputation is read till it is read at least twice. You can easily test the truth of this by reading again any classic.

ARNOLD BENNETT

An unliterary man may be defined as one who reads books once only. There is hope for a man who has never read Malory or Boswell or *Tristram Shandy* or Shakespeare's *Sonnets:* but what can you do with a man who says he 'has read' them, meaning he has read them once, and thinks that settles the matter?

C. S. LEWIS

A good book improves with rereading—as the light from furthest planets takes longest to reach our earth. The reverse is also true, for as we discover more and more in Shakespeare, so the contemporary poet who delighted us at first has become extinct when we re-open him in a few years' time—his fairy gold turned to withered leaves.

AUGUSTUS RALLI

Repeat reading for me shares a few things with hot-water bottles and thumb-sucking: comfort, familiarity, the recurrence of the expected.

MARGARET ATWOOD

There was going to be a storm and it was a perfect night for rereading *Jane Eyre*. Bailey had finished his chores and was already behind the stove with Mark Twain . . .

MAYA ANGELOU

Reading books is good,
Rereading good books is better.

LAWRENCE CLARK POWELL

One cannot *read* a book: one can only reread it. A good reader, a major reader, an active and creative reader is a rereader. . . . When we read a book for the first time the very process of laboriously moving our eyes from left to right, line after line, page after page, this complicated physical work upon the book, the very process of learning in terms of space and time what the book is about, this stands between us and artistic appreciation.

VLADIMIR NABOKOV

I too feel the need to read the books I have always read . . . but at every rereading I seem to be reading a new book, for the first time. Is it I who keep changing and seeing new things of which I was not previously aware: Or is reading a construction that assumes form, assembling a great number of variables, and therefore something that cannot be repeated twice according to the same pattern?

ITALO CALVINO

[I]t is only at the beginning of an attempt at a second reading or at the end of it, and only then, if one is self-assured, that one can see whether a book was not really worth reading the first time; one tells by how alterable the truth in it seems in this more familiar light and how effective the book remains or, contrarily, how amazingly empty of meaning it now shows itself to be.

HAROLD BRODKEY

There's a paradox in rereading. You read the first time for rediscovery: an encounter with the confirming emotions. But you reread for discovery: you go to the known to figure out the workings of the unknown, the why of the familiar how.

CYNTHIA OZICK

Rereading can be ... a humility-inducing activity, when, on rereading, one learns that the first time around with a book, one's politics or fantasies or personal anxieties were in fact doing most of the work. Rereading books first read when young, one is inclined to weep for the naif one not so long ago was. And while at it one discovers, if one gets to reread the same book twenty years hence, one is even one now.

JOSEPH EPSTEIN

There is no reason why the same man should like the same books at eighteen and forty-eight.

EZRA POUND

The return to a favorite novel is generally tied up with changes in oneself that must be counted as improvements, but have the feel of losses. It is like going back to a favorite house, country, person; nothing is where it belongs, including one's heart.

MARY MCCARTHY

It is probably a mistake to go back to the decisive books of one's youth. They are causes; the reader has long since become, in part, their effect. Clear vision is just not possible.

SVEN BIRKERTS

Ordinary books are like meteors. Each of them has only one moment, a moment when it soars screaming like the phoenix, all its pages aflame. For that single moment we love them ever after, although they soon turn to ashes. With bitter resignation we sometimes wander late at night through the extinct pages that tell their stone dead messages like wooden rosary beads.

BRUNO SCHULZ (*The Book*)

The best writing . . . is that which engages us both intellectually and aesthetically even as it disturbs our customary way of perceiving the world. It invites and sustains subsequent readings.

STANLEY W. LINDBERG

Poetry is . . . to be read and reread till it reveals its secrets. It is better to read one poem ten times than to read ten poems once.

LEO STEIN

BOOKS AS FRIENDS

Good books, like good friends, are few and chosen;
the more select, the more enjoyable.
LOUISA MAY ALCOTT

The books I read are the ones I knew and loved when
I was a young man and to which I return as you do to
friends: the Old Testament, Dickens, Conrad, Cervantes—*Don Quixote*. I read that every year, as some
do the Bible. . . . I've read these books so often that I
don't always begin at page one and read on to the
end. I just read one scene, or about one character just
as you'd meet and talk to a friend for a few minutes.
WILLIAM FAULKNER

I hold my books up to memory's light, faces gleam,
there are whispers from long ago belonging to old
friends. . . . I open the books; the characters stretch
and pull me back in.
JILL ROBINSON

Ah! the books that one will never read again. They
gave delight, perchance something more; they left a
perfume in the memory; but life has passed them by
forever. . . . Perhaps when I lie waiting for the end,
some of these lost books will come into my wander-
ing thoughts, and I shall remember them as friends to
whom I owed a kindness—friends passed upon the
way.
GEORGE GISSING

Books have been my most dependable friends and my unfailing source of pleasure, a mainstay, and the better part of whatever brains I have. It is quite impossible for me to imagine a life without books; not as a substitute for it, but as a continuous and refreshing enrichment.

ASHLEY MONTAGUE

When I see books that I have read on library shelves, it is like running into an old friend on the street. I often take the book down and browse through it, even though I have no intention of checking it out of the library and reading it once again. . . . Like friends, these books have gone into the making of whatever and whoever I am.

KEVIN STARR

There is one respect in which the book is the best of possible friends. A book never bores you because you can always lay it down before it becomes a bore.

LYMAN ABBOTT

One can read to make friends, friends who are never not at home; never out of temper; never false. Perhaps all my critical judgments are eccentrically personal. A book, to me, means a person, rather than a thing. There are authors that I love better than all but a handful of people I have known in the flesh; authors that I loathe and despise with an intensity that, fortunately, no living acquaintance has ever aroused.

F. L. LUCAS

An ever-increasing number of people will discover that books will give them all the pleasures of social life and none of its intolerable tedium. At present people in search of pleasure naturally tend to congregate in large herds and to make a noise; in future their natural tendency will be to seek solitude and quiet. The proper study of mankind is books.

ALDOUS HUXLEY (*Crome Yellow*)

Reading is a private act, like reflection.... In reading, as in the best teaching, there is a simple equation between two persons: opposite the reader is the writer, who has had also to engage in a private act.

WILLIAM JOVANOVICH

Books are like individuals; you know at once if they are going to create a sense within the sense, to fever, to madden you in blood and brain, or if they will merely leave you indifferent, or irritable, having unpleasantly disturbed sweet intimate musings as might a draught from an open window. Many are the reasons for love, but I confess I only love woman or book, when it is as a voice of conscience, never heard before, heard suddenly, a voice I am at once endearingly intimate with.

GEORGE MOORE

Reading for experience is the only reading that justifies excitement. Reading for facts is necessary but the less said about it in public the better. Reading for distraction is like taking medicine. We do it, but it is nothing to be proud of. But reading for experience is transforming. Neither man nor woman is ever quite the same again after the experience of a book that enters deeply into life....

HENRY SEIDEL CANBY

Reading a good book is not much different from a love affair, from love, complete with shyness and odd assertions of power and of independence and with many sorts of incompleteness in the experience. One can marry the book: reread it, add it to one's life, live with it.

HAROLD BRODKEY

There are books that create an exhilaration close to ecstasy. The reader feels like a tall building in darkness to which the owners return and, floor by floor, begin switching on the lights.

BLANCHE D'ALPUGET

Reading is the work of the alert mind, is demanding, and under ideal conditions produces finally a sort of ecstasy. As in the sexual experience, there are never more than two persons present in the act of reading— the writer, who is the impregnator, and the reader, who is the respondent. This gives the experience of reading a sublimity and power unequalled by any other form of communication.

E. B. WHITE

A book is meant not only to be read, but to haunt you, to importune you like a lover or a parent, to stick in your teeth like a piece of gristle.

ANATOLE BROYARD

WHAT TO READ

The best guide to books is a book itself. It clasps hands with a thousand other books.

MAURICE FRANCIS EGAN

I have never cared to read books on subjects that were in no way my concern, and I still cannot bring myself to read books of entertainment or instruction about people or places that mean nothing to me. I do not want to know the history of Hungary or the manners and customs of the Eskimos. . . .

W. SOMERSET MAUGHAM

I seek in books only to give myself pleasure by honest amusement; or if I study, I seek only the learning that treats of the knowledge of myself and instructs me in how to die well and live well.

MICHEL DE MONTAIGNE

I can read anything which I call a *book*. There are things in that shape which I cannot allow for such. In this catalogue of *books which are not books—biblia a-biblia*——I reckon court calendars, directories, pocket books, draught boards, bound and lettered on the back, scientific treatises, almanacs, statutes at large . . . and all those volumes which "no gentleman's library should be without."

CHARLES LAMB

But how few, after all, the books that *are* books! Charles Lamb let his kind heart master him when he made that too brief list of books that *aren't*. Book is an honorable title, not to be conferred lightly. . . . The test is, whether it was worth reading. Had the author something to set forth? And had he the specific gift for setting it forth in written words? And did he use this rather rare gift conscientiously and to the full? And were his words well and appropriately printed and bound? If you can say Yes to these questions, then only, I submit, is the title of 'book' deserved.

MAX BEERBOHM

There is a frailty in man which compels him, in spite of himself, to read when once he has learnt to read, just as if compelled to smoke when once he has broken himself in, with much nausea, through his teens, to the beastly habit of smoking. In spite of yourself you will find yourself picking up books, opening them at random and glancing at a line or two of the stodge within.

HILAIRE BELLOC

Except a living man, there is nothing more wonderful than a book!—a message to us from the dead—from human souls whom we never saw, who lived perhaps thousands of miles away: and yet these, on those little sheets of paper, speak to us, amuse us, vivify us, teach us, comfort us, open their hearts to us as brothers. . . .

CHARLES KINGSLEY

All the best experience of humanity, folded, saved, freighted to us here! Some of these tiny ships we call Old and New Testament, Homer, Aeschylus, Plato, Juvenal, etc. Precious minims!

WALT WHITMAN

A man should begin with his own times. He should become acquainted first of all with the world in which he is living and participating. He should not be afraid of reading too much or too little. He should take his reading as he does his food or his exercise. The good reader will gravitate to the good books. He will discover from his contemporaries what is inspiring or fecundating, or merely enjoyable, in past literature. He should have the pleasure of making these discoveries on his own, in his own way. What has worth, charm, beauty, wisdom, cannot be lost or forgotten. But things can lose all value, all charm and appeal, if one is dragged to them by the scalp.

HENRY MILLER

The fact that a book is famous is enough to scare off some people who, if they had the courage to open the pages, would find there delight and profit. We make the mistake of fearing that the immortal things of art must be approached through special studies. . . .

JOHN ERSKINE

I must confess that even now when I pick up for the first time one of the so-called classics, I get an unexpected and bewildered start of pleasure in discovering life and beauty within the ornate and chill tomb of righteous appreciation.

WILLIAM WHITMAN

A true classic . . . is an author who . . . speaks to all in a style of his own, which happens also to be that of common speech, a style new but without neologisms, new and old at the same time, easily acceptable to any epoch.

CHARLES SAINTE-BEUVE

He who is not familiarized with the finest passages of the finest writers will one day be mortified to observe that his best thoughts are their indifferent ones.

ISAAC DISRAELI

The sum of it all is: read what you like, because you like it, seeking no other reason and no other profit than the experience of reading. If you enjoy the experience it is well; but whether you enjoy it or not the experience is worth having.

HOLBROOK JACKSON

The book which you read from a sense of duty, or because for any reason you must, does not commonly make friends with you. It may happen that it will yield you an unexpected delight, but this will be in its own unentreated way in spite of your good intentions.

WILLIAM DEAN HOWELLS

The books that a man needs to know in order to 'get his bearings,' in order to have a sound judgment of any bit of writing that may come before him, are very few. The list is so short, indeed, that one wonders that people, professional writers in particular, are willing to leave them ignored and to continue dangling in mid-chaos emitting the most imbecile estimates, and often vitiating their whole lifetime's production.

EZRA POUND

It does not matter how many, but how good, books you have.

LUCIUS ANNAEUS SENECA

Life being very short, and the quiet hours of it few, we ought to waste none of them in reading valueless books.

JOHN RUSKIN

If a man wants to read good books, he must make a point of avoiding bad ones; for life is short, and time and energy limited.

ARTHUR SCHOPENHAUER

Many people lose a great deal of time by reading: for
they read frivolous and idle books, such as the absurd
romances of the two last centuries; where characters,
that never existed, are insipidly displayed, and senti-
ments that were never felt, pompously described . . .
that nourishes and improves the mind just as much as
whipped cream the body.

EARL OF CHESTERFIELD

To have read the latest literary wonders may enable
one to prattle at tea-parties; but, had one only waited
a year, they might all have blown away, like last year's
leaves. And is it kind to one's mind to cram it
higgledy-piggledy with whatever is just out; much as
if a monthly van came and shot pell-mell into one's
cellar sardines and skipping-ropes, sugar and seed-
potatoes, coal and looking-glasses?

F. L. LUCAS

With so many fine books to be read, so much to be
studied and known, there is no need to bore ourselves
with this rubbish.

EDMUND WILSON

As for the literary pundits, the high priests of the
Temple of Letters, it is interesting and helpful occasionally, for an acolyte to swing them a good hard
one with an incense-burner, and cut and run, for a
change, to something outside the rubrics.

H. W. TOMLINSON

In literature, vulgarity is preferable to nullity, just as grocer's port is preferable to distilled water.

W. H. AUDEN

I would rather read something inferior than nothing at all. Sometimes the reader is not interested in being enlightened, uplifted or even entertained. He wants merely to escape for a brief interval from the world which is suddenly too much with him.

JEROME WEIDMAN

While civilization remains such that one needs distraction from time to time, "light" literature has its appointed place.

GEORGE ORWELL

There is nothing more disgusting than the taste of a rotten book and nothing like the taste of a good book; nothing like it, nothing.

PHILIP ROTH

We have times and moods and tenses of black depression and despair and general mental discomfort.... [T]hat is just the time when a man is peculiarly accessible to the influence of a book ...; and moreover, that is just the time when he naturally and instinctively does not want anything of a mind-taxing soul-stirring nature. Then is the time to fall back on the books that neither pretend to be nor are accepted as masterpieces, but books whose tone and temper soothe your trouble for the time being.

RUDYARD KIPLING

An old book is always comforting; it speaks to us from a distance, we can listen or not, and when suddenly mighty words flare up, we take them not as we would from a book of today, from an author with such and such a name, but as though at first hand, as we take the cry of a gull or a ray of sunlight.

HERMANN HESSE

There remains more life in some books dead a thousand years than in much that passes for living, but remains really as futile as froth-blowing.

F. L. LUCAS

I cannot understand the rage manifested by the greater part of the world for reading new books.... If I have not read a book before, it is, to all intents and purposes, new to me, whether it was printed yesterday or three hundred years ago.

WILLIAM HAZLITT

The old hunger to know what the immortals thought has given place to a far more tolerant curiosity to know what our own generation is thinking. . . . And soon we develop another taste, unsatisfied by the great—not a valuable taste, perhaps, but certainly a very pleasant possession—the taste for bad books. . . . We know which authors can be trusted to produce yearly (for happily they are prolific) a [book] which affords us indescribable pleasure. We owe a great deal to bad books; indeed, we come to count their authors and their heroes among those figures who play so large a part in our silent life.

VIRGINIA WOOLF

The most useful help to reading is to know what we should not read, what we can keep out from that small cleared spot in the overgrown jungle of 'information,' the corner of which we call our ordered patch of fruit-bearing-knowledge.

FREDERIC HARRISON

Few negative pleasures are as exhilarating to the bookish as reading a persuasive review whose gravamen is that one needn't bother reading a prolific writer whose many works one has had a bad conscience about not hitherto having read.

JOSEPH EPSTEIN

I do not believe much in any set program of reading in our idle hours. . . . I prefer to trust to the charm of chance, which constantly gives us glimpses of style or splendour on some unexpected page that we might never have included in the programme of a study-circle for ourselves or for anybody else.

SIR IAN MALCOLM

Literature has many mansions and excellence is found in many forms—some of them unassuming and even fugitive. . . . The true reader allows himself a balanced diet and moves easily through the categories from philosophy to humor—and he is, or ought to be, equally annoyed if either of them fails to give him the *literary* thrill—the thrill of good words—on top of philosophical knowledge or hilarious entertainment.

JACQUES BARZUN

It is desultory reading that develops one's taste. It is fortunate that when we are young we are unfocussed.

VAN WYCK BROOKS

My education was the liberty I had to read indiscriminately and all the time with my eye's hanging out.

DYLAN THOMAS

What the Boy chiefly dabbled in was natural history and fairytales, and he just took them as they came, in a sandwichy sort of way, without making any distinctions; and really his course of reading strikes me as rather sensible.

KENNETH GRAHAME (*The Reluctant Dragon*)

If "the open road" is the way to take in journeying through life, surely the same applies to reading. Let it be an adventure! Let it *happen!*

HENRY MILLER

Read at whim! read at whim!

RANDALL JARRELL

MYSTERIES

Detective stories help reassure us in the belief that the universe, underneath it all, is rational. They're small celebrations of order and reason in an increasingly disordered world.

P. D. JAMES

When I'm working on a serious and solid book . . . I read about a detective novel a day. It's the best legal dope in the world. It makes you feel good until the next morning you can work again.

MARY LEE SETTLE

I read two [detective stories] a week in bed at night: can't concentrate on much else then. . . . To me they are a great solace, a sort of mental knitting, where it doesn't matter if you drop a stitch.

RUPERT HART-DAVIS

Mystery fiction is, after all, a substitute for tranquilizers, strong drink, and bad, if diverting, companions. One slips into bed . . . onto the train . . . into the chair in the sickroom . . . and is suddenly transported to a place where light fights dark and wins. When the story's over, one is left without a hangover, without remorse. Can any other opiate make that claim?

MARY CANTWELL

The reading of detective stories is simply a kind of vice that, for silliness and minor harmfulness, ranks somewhere between smoking and crossword puzzles.
EDMUND WILSON

I once compared the detective story to a welder's mask which enables both writer and reader to handle dangerously hot materials. . . . Traditional detective fiction offers us the assurance that in spite of all its horrors—the speckled band in Conan Doyle, the dead girl thrust up the chimney in Poe's *Rue Morgue*—the world makes sense and can be understood.
ROSS MACDONALD

Even the . . . detective story can be good if it expresses something of the delight in sinister possibilities—the healthy lust for darkness and terror which may come upon us any night in walking down a dark lane.
G. K. CHESTERTON

Quinn had been a devoted reader of mystery novels. He knew that most of them were poorly written, that most could not stand up to even the vaguest sort of examination, but still, it was the form that appealed to him, and it was the rare unspeakably bad mystery he would refuse to read. . . .
PAUL AUSTER (*City of Glass*)

The detective story is the normal recreation of noble minds.
PHILIP GUEDALLA

Anyone who hopes that in time it may be possible to abolish war should give serious thought to the problem of satisfying harmlessly the instincts that we inherit from long generations of savages. For my part I find a sufficient outlet in detective stories, where I alternately identify myself with the murderer and the huntsman-detective.

BERTRAND RUSSELL

Sublimation is the retail draining-off, as it were, of our malevolence upon substitute objects. And what a world of substitute objects books provide! . . . When men know not whom to shoot, they shoot they know not whom. It is better to take it out on men in Whodunits than to murder your neighbor or your boss.

T. V. SMITH

A good detective story is the answer to Lowell's question, 'What is so rare as a day in June?'

FRANKLIN DELANO ROOSEVELT

My purpose is to entertain myself first and other people secondly.

JOHN D. MACDONALD

Life is short and the number of books is appalling. It is a kind of insanity to satiate oneself with short sensation-tales and detective-tales and leave untouched the great, slow, deep-breathed classics.

JOHN COWPER POWYS

My theory is that people who don't like mystery stories are anarchists.

REX STOUT

For some reason, I can't read mysteries any more. Now I can understand why people say, 'I never read mysteries.' I don't think they should say that to me, but mysteries are boring.

MARTHA GRIMES

The danger that may really threaten [crime fiction] is that soon there will be more writers than readers.

JACQUES BARZUN

POETRY

There seem to be very few people who read poetry at the finger tips, so to speak. . . . Most people read it listening for echoes because the echoes are familiar to them. They wade through it the way a boy wades through water, feeling with his toes for the bottom: the echoes are the bottom.

WALLACE STEVENS

After reading a passage of true poetry of our time, whether in verse or prose (but the most powerful impressions come from verse), one can say, even in these prosaic times, what Sterne said about a smile, that it adds a thread to the short canvas of our life.

GIACOMO LEOPARDI

Poetry should surprise by a fine excess and not by singularity—it should strike the reader as a wording of his own highest thoughts, and appear almost a remembrance.

JOHN KEATS

Poetry is, as living art should be, made for performance and that its performance is not reading with the eye but loud, leisurely poetical (not rhetorical) recitation, with long rests, long dwells on the rhyme and other marked syllables, and so on.

GERARD MANLEY HOPKINS

Of all literary pleasures, the reading of a poem is the highest and purest. Only pure lyric poetry can sometimes achieve the perfection, the ideal form wholly permeated by life and feeling, that is otherwise the secret of music.

HERMANN HESSE

[I]f you cannot read poetry easily and naturally and joyfully, you are cut off from much of the great literature of the past, some of the good literature of the present.

RANDALL JARRELL

You'll accidentally find
  in barrows of books
wrought-iron lines of long-buried poems,
handle them
  with the care that respects
ancient
  but terrible weapons ...

V. V. MAYAKOVSKY (from *At the Top of My Voice*)

Poetry can save the world. I'm a real believer in its power of healing and transforming. I wish more people read it ... Poetry is probably as close as I would get to religious feeling. I think poetry makes the world stand still.

CAROL MUSKE

You enjoy poetry more if you set aside a stretch of time for reading in which you don't expect to be interrupted; most poems begin to yield their full meaning only after several careful, unhurried readings. And try also to keep an open mind as you read: "listen" to what the poem is trying to tell you in its own language.

RICHARD ELLMANN & ROBERT O'CLAIR

The most seasoned reader . . . does not bother about understanding; not, at least, at first. I know that some of the poetry to which I am most devoted is poetry which I did not understand at first reading; some is poetry which I am not sure I understand yet. . . .

T. S. ELIOT

It is better to read a difficult poem a dozen times, than to read it once and then have it explained to you. In the one case the process of re-creation takes place and in the other it does not.

LEO STEIN

The impact of poetry is so hard and direct that for the moment there is no other sensation except that of the poem itself. . . . Our being for the moment is centered and constricted, as in any violent shock of personal emotion. Afterwards, it is true, the sensation begins to spread in wider rings through our minds; remoter senses are touched; these begin to sound and to comment and we are aware of echoes and reflections.

VIRGINIA WOOLF

Poetry might become the fashion—a real danger because the poets need an audience not fitful and superficial, but loyal and sincere.
HARRIET MONROE

Poetry . . . arouses people and shapes their minds. . . . It is the golden treasury in which our values are preserved.
NADEZHDA MANDELSTAM

I want to . . . read poems filled with terror and music that changes laws and lives.
LEONARD COHEN

Ink runs from the corners of my mouth
There is no happiness like mine.
I have been eating poetry.
MARK STRAND (from *Eating Poetry*)

The joys
Of poetry, for those who
Appreciate them, increase with
Time and familiarity,
Their richness never ends in
Satiety.
OU YANG HISU (from *Reading the Poems of an Absent Friend* tr. Kenneth Rexroth)

I, too, dislike it: there are things that are important
    beyond all this fiddle.
    Reading it, however, with perfect contempt for
    it, one discovers in it after all, a place for the gen-
    uine.

   MARIANNE MOORE (from *Poetry*)

When power leads man toward arrogance, poetry reminds him of his limitations. When power narrows
the areas of man's concerns, poetry reminds him of
the richness and diversity of his experience. When
power corrupts, poetry cleanses, for art establishes the
basic human truths which must serve as the touch-
stones of our judgment.

   JOHN F. KENNEDY

If after I read a poem the world looks like that poem
for 24 hrs. or so I'm sure it's a good one.

   ELIZABETH BISHOP

WHERE TO READ

There are favorable hours for reading a book, as for writing it.

HENRY WADSWORTH LONGFELLOW

Books are . . . a delight at home, and no hindrance abroad; companions at night, in travelling, in the country.

CICERO

There are rainy afternoons in the country in autumn, and stormy days in winter, when one's work outdoors is finished and after wet clothes have been changed for dry, the rocking-chair in front of the open wood-fire simply demands an accompanying book.

THEODORE ROOSEVELT

The reader's song is of the drawn curtain and the fire-flicker, the subdued light of the lamp and the wild rush of the wind without. At such a time his books are doubly friends; they partake of his security from the raging inclemency, and share the hospitality which friend proffers friend in storm-time and in need.

J. ROGER REES

Have you any right to read, especially novels, until you have exhausted the best part of the day in some employment that is called practical?

CHARLES DUDLEY WARNER

A little before you sleep read something that is exquisite, and worth remembering; and, when you awake in the morning, call yourself to an account for it.

DESIDERIUS ERASMUS

While one's body rests itself, one's mind remains alert, and, when the time for sleep comes at last, it passes into unconsciousness, tranquilized and sweetened with thought and pleasantly weary with healthy exercise. One awakens, too, next morning, with, so to say, a very pleasant taste of meditation in the mouth.

RICHARD LEGALLIENNE

And, sometimes, at home, in my bed, long after dinner, the last hours of the evening would also shelter my reading.

MARCEL PROUST

To read in bed is to draw around us invisible, noiseless curtains. Then at last we are in a room of our own and are ready to burrow back, back, back to that private life of the imagination we all led as children and to whose secret satisfactions so many of us have mislaid the key.

CLIFTON FADIMAN

At home when I have shut my door and the town is in bed—and I know that nothing, not even the dawn, can disturb me in my curtains: only the slow crumbling of the coals in the fire.

T. E. LAWRENCE

I cannot sleep unless I am surrounded by books.

JORGE LUIS BORGES

There are a few books which go with midnight, solitude, and a candle. It is much easier to say what does not please us than what is exactly right. The book must be, anyhow, something benedictory by a sinning fellow-man. Cleverness would be repellant at such an hour.

H. M. TOMLINSON

The hour before sleep is the best time for the rereading of old favorites. You know precisely where you are and what to expect, yet you may have the pleasure of coming upon a particularly good passage the full flavor of which had previously escaped you. There can be a tinge of excitement in that, but not so strong as to set your mind racing.

J. DONALD ADAMS

The habit of reading novels in bed is universal, even among bishops and judges, and it is the modern more or less ephemeral novel which is utilized in this way, because, no doubt, it need not be taken too seriously and can be "wolfed" with a clear (literary) conscience.

E. B. OSBORN

A wonderful thing about a book, in contrast to a computer screen, is that you can take it to bed with you.

DANIEL J. BOORSTIN

Having created a habit of night reading, my life is a search for longer and longer books. I do not want them to end. . . . But the modern novel, which tends to be subtle rather than profound, entertaining rather than instructive, unmoral and reflective of our chaos, is too disturbing a companion for the long, despondent hours of night. I read them by daylight.

OLIVIA MANNING

Borrow, therefore, of these golden morning hours, and bestow them on a book.

EARL OF BEDFORD

Rise early, and at the same hour every morning, how late soever you may have sat up the night before. This secures you an hour or two, at least, of reading or reflection before the common interruptions of the morning begin.

EARL OF CHESTERFIELD

Early on weekday mornings, I'd read in my bed. I'd feel a mysterious comfort then, reading in the dawn quiet—the blue-gray silence interrupted by the occasional churning of the refrigerator motor a few rooms away or the more distant sounds of a city bus beginning its run.

RICHARD RODRIGUEZ

My mother read to me in the big bedroom in the mornings, when we were in her rocker together, which ticked in rhythm as we rocked, as though we had a cricket accompanying the story.

EUDORA WELTY

Early morning was a time he enjoyed reading. His mind was alert, the attention span seemed to continue indefinitely, right until he remembered about having to go to school. It was a nice time, a peaceful time. There was something about giving your best to the things you liked the best.

JAMES KELMAN (*Disaffection*)

After breakfast he picked up a book and settled down by his long front bedroom window to read; this had been his morning custom for nearly fifty years. . . . He read poetry for the most part, and he read chiefly for sound, taking pleasure in the pattern of the words as they formed and echoed deep within his brain. . . . It was an incongruous picture: the aging political boss, up shortly after dawn, preparing for the daily war of the wards by reading a volume of verse.

EDWIN O'CONNOR (*The Last Hurrah*)

My custom is to undress, and sit on the rocks, reading Herodotus, until the perspiration has subsided, and then to leap from the edge of the rock into this fountain—a practice in the hot weather excessively refreshing.

PERCY BYSSHE SHELLEY

For a whole day together, have I lain
Down by thy side, O Derwent! murmuring stream,
On the hot stones, and in the glaring sun,
And there have read, devouring as I read,
Defrauding the day's glory, desperate!

WILLIAM WORDSWORTH

Then I went indoors, brought out a loaf,
	Half a cheese, and a bottle of Chablis;
Lay on the grass and forgot the loaf
	Over a jolly chapter of Rabelais.

ROBERT BROWNING

A Book of Verses underneath the Bough,
    A Jug of Wine, a Loaf of Bread—and Thou
Beside me singing in the Wilderness—
    Oh, Wilderness were Paradise enow!
  OMAR KHAYYAM (tr. Edward Fitzgerald)

Who is more happy, when, with heart's content,
Fatigued he sinks into some pleasant lair
Of wavy grass, and reads a debonair
And gentle tale of love and languishment?
  JOHN KEATS

As my walking companion in the country I was so un-English as, on the whole, to prefer my pocket Milton, which I carried for twenty years, to the not unbeloved bull-terrier "Trimmer," who accompanied me for five: for Milton never fidgeted, frightened horses, ran after sheep, or got run over by a goods-van.
  SAMUEL PALMER

We'd go for walks and picnics, taking books in baskets, and sit under trees and read. I now live once more in the same part of the country which isn't much changed since I was a child; I can still find the spot where David Copperfield first met Mr. Murdstone and the tree where the Knight of the Leopard had his picnic with Saladin.
  JOAN AIKEN

For lying in your backyard hammock . . . make sure
the book will provide at least two hours of entertainment, otherwise it's not worth the struggle to get
comfortable in a hammock—nor the inevitable tum-
ble when you want out.

SYLVIA SACHS

I seldom read in beaches or in gardens. You can't read
by two lights at once, the light of day and the light of
the book. You should read by electric light, the room
in shadow, and only the page lit up.

MARGUERITE DURAS

[I]f we are traveling, we sometimes need a quiet rest-
ing place for the spirit; not an intellectual motel, but a
sanctuary—somewhere to rest, and live for ourselves,
and think. Physically, it is not always possible to pro-
cure this. Mentally, it can be assured, if we have something to read.

GILBERT HIGHET

If you are to have but one book with you upon a journey, let it be a book of science, [for] when you have
read through a book of entertainment, you know it,
and it can do no more for you; but a book of science
is inexhaustible.

SAMUEL JOHNSON

Shipboard reading—it falls into a category generally despised. The usual view is that reading for a journey must be of the lightest and shallowest, mere foolery to pass the time. . . . Perhaps the conditions of life on shipboard, at once removed from the everyday and full of excitement, produce a mental and nervous condition in which silliness disgusts us less than usual.
THOMAS MANN

I know of nothing cosier than a bunk in a boat crossing a calm sea. With a pleasant sense of adventure at the back of your mind you can read in your little lair as snug as a wren in its nest amid winter snow.
PHILLIP GLAZEBROOK

On Board Ship: Reading Yuan Chen's Poems

I take your poems in my hand and read them
    beside the candle;
The poems are finished; the candle is low;
    dawn not yet come.
With sore eyes by the guttering candle still
    I sit in the dark,
Listening to waves that, driven by the wind,
    strike the prow of the ship.
PO CHU-I (tr. Arthur Waley)

As far back as I can remember, on unnumbered waters of the world and in all manifestations of the sea's unending repertory of moods, whether placid as some inland lake or stormy enough to roll one's body back and forth, port and starboard, with the ship herself while one clutched hard the volume, I have read a half hour before bed, sitting up in my bunk, before marking my place and reaching up and snapping off the overhead light.

WILLIAM BRINKLEY (*The Last Ship*)

The best time for reading . . . is when one is on a train travelling alone. With strangers roundabout, and unfamiliar scenery passing by the window (at which you glance now and again) the endearing and convoluted life coming out of the pages possesses its own peculiar and imprinting effects.

ALAN SILLITOE

[H]aphazard meetings with books sometimes present them under conditions hopelessly unfavorable, as when I first encountered Whitman's 'Leaves of Grass' for the first time on my first voyage in an Axorian barque; and it inspires to this day a slight sense of nausea.

THOMAS WENTWORTH HIGGINSON

READERS

[Alexander the Great] was naturally a great lover of all kinds of learning and reading; . . . he constantly laid Homer's *Iliad* . . . with his dagger under his pillow, declaring that he esteemed it a perfect portable treasure of all military virtue and knowledge.

PLUTARCH

Sir, he hath never fed on the dainties that are bred in a book; he hath not eat paper, as it were; he hath not drunk ink; his intellect is not replenished; he is only an animal, only sensibled in the duller parts.

WILLIAM SHAKESPEARE (*Love's Labours Lost*)

He gave himself up so wholly to the reading of romances that a-nights he would pore on until it was day, and a-days he would read on until it was night; and thus be sleeping little and reading much the moisture of his brain was exhausted to that degree that at last he lost the use of his reason.

MIGUEL DE CERVANTES SAAVEDRA (*Don Quixote*)

If all thy pipes of wine were fill'd with books,
Made of the barks of trees, or mysteries writ
In old moth-eaten vellum, he would sip thy cellar
Quite dry, and still be thirsty. Then, for's diet,
He eats and digests more volumes at a meal,
Than there would be larks (though the sky should fall)
Devour'd in a month in Paris.
   JOHN FLETCHER

At this day, as much company as I have kept, and as much as I love it, I love reading better.
   ALEXANDER POPE

In the old days I think it must have been easy to acquire the habit of reading. People stayed for months in the same house without stirring from it even for a night. The opportunities for reading were so many, and the opportunities for doing other things were comparatively so few, that the habit of reading must almost have been forced upon them.
   VISCOUNT GREY

If the crowns of all the kingdoms of the Empire were laid down at my feet in exchange for my books and my love of reading, I would spurn them all.
   FRANÇOIS FÉNELON

'The Mysteries of Udolpho' when I had once begun it, I could not lay down again;—I remember finishing it in two days—my hair standing on end the whole time.

JANE AUSTEN (*Northanger Abbey*)

Books are becoming everything to me. If I had at this moment my choice of life, I would bury myself in one of those immense libraries that we saw together at the universities, and would never pass a waking hour without a book before me.

LORD MACAULAY

Much as I love my calling, I am a true bookworm, and hope on my return to find, about once a month, a whole day for a Great Read! . . . I, in a dull, pattering, gusty December day, which forbids our wishes to rove beyond the tops of the chimney-pots—a good fire, a sofa strewed with books, a reading friend, and above all, a locked door, forbidding impertinent intrusion.

SAMUEL PALMER

I am never long, even in the society of her I love, without yearning for the company of my lamp and my library.

LORD BYRON

I cannot live without books.

THOMAS JEFFERSON

The farm boys in their evenings at Jones's store in Gentryville talked about how Abe Lincoln was always reading, digging into books, stretching out flat on his stomach in front of the fireplace, studying till midnight and past midnight ... The next thing Abe would be reading books between the plow handles, it seemed to them.

CARL SANDBURG (*Abraham Lincoln: The Prairie Years*)

[Old Sorel] might perhaps have forgiven Julien his slender build, unsuited to heavy labor and so different from that of his older boys, but that mania for reading was abominable to him: he himself did not know how to read.

STENDHAL (*The Red and the Black*)

A little peaceful home
Bounds all my wants and wishes; add to this
My book and friend, and this is happiness

FRANCESCO DI RIOJA

At the time I was literally starving in London, when it seemed impossible that I should ever gain a living by my pen, how many days have I spent at the British Museum, reading as disinterestedly as if I had been without a care! It astounds me to remember that, having breakfasted on dry bread, and carrying in my pocket another piece of bread to serve for dinner, I settled myself at a desk in the great Reading Room with books before me which by no possibility could be a source of immediate profit.

GEORGE GISSING (*The Private Papers of Henry Ryecroft*)

To avoid wasting a precious half-hour, I used to take bread and chocolate with me and ate them openly at midday in the reading-room. Around me other readers, shame-faced and short of money, were also eating bread, but breaking off the pieces in their pockets. Twelve noon was the signal for a vast chorus of munching.

HENRY DE MONTHERLANT

Without sufficient money for a meal I have spent the few pence I possessed to obtain from a library one of Scott's novels, and, reading it, forgot hunger and cold, and felt myself rich and happy.

HANS CHRISTIAN ANDERSEN

I like books. I was born and bred among them, and have the easy feeling, when I get into their presence, that a stable-boy has among horses.

OLIVER WENDELL HOLMES

What better occupation, really than to spend the evening at the fireside with a book, with the wind beating on the windows and the lamp burning bright? . . . Without moving, you walk through the countries you see in your mind's eye; and your thoughts, caught up in the story, stop at the details or rush through the plot. You pretend you're the characters and feel it's your own heart beating beneath their costumes.

GUSTAVE FLAUBERT (*Madame Bovary*)

He did not think of these books as something invented to beguile the idle hour, but as living creatures, caught in the very behaviour of living—surprised behind their misleading severity of form and phrase. He was eaves-dropping upon the past, being let into the great world that had plunged and glittered and sumptuously sinned long before little Western towns were dreamed of. Those rapt evenings beside the lamp gave him a long perspective, influenced his conception of the people about him, made him know just what he wished his own relations with those people to be.

WILLA CATHER (*A Lost Lady*)

If, somewhere outside this world, an account has been kept of the number of hours I have wasted in the reading of novels, it would point inevitably to the conclusion that, for a very long time, I preferred fiction to reality. I remember how, when I first settled in Paris, as soon as I could escape from the Ecole des Chartes, and from all that turned young students into slaves, I never budged from my fire except to eat a hurried meal, and, even then, did not lay aside my book.

FRANÇOIS MAURIAC

A ravening appetite in him demanded that he read everything that had ever been written about human experience. He read no more from pleasure—the thought that other books were waiting for him tore at his heart forever. He pictured himself as tearing the entrails from a book as from a fowl.

THOMAS WOLFE (*Of Time and the River*)

Reading grew into a passion. . . . I gave myself over to each novel without reserve, without trying to criticize it; it was enough for me to see and feel something different. And for me, everything was something different. Reading was like a drug, a dope. The novels created moods in which I lived for days.

RICHARD WRIGHT

Not unusually, my only refuge was in books. For some reason my parents encouraged this appetite. Had they known how subversive it was, they would have denied me, no differently than they punished me for breaking rules by prohibiting nougats and cakes. . . . My best year was my tenth. I read three hundred and sixty-five books. It was a year of recurrent illness.

ARTHUR A. COHEN (*An Admirable Woman*)

Bastian Balthazar Bux's passion was books. If you have never spent the whole afternoon with burning ears and rumpled hair, forgetting the world around you over a book, forgetting cold and hunger. . . .

MICHAEL ENDE (*The Neverending Story*)

Those who retain all through life a deep commitment to literacy harbor in their unconscious some residue of their earlier conviction that reading is an art permitting access to magic worlds, although very few of them are aware that they subconsciously believe this to be so.

BRUNO BETTLEHEIM & KAREN ZELAN

She reads anything and everything and even now hates to be disturbed and above all however often she has read a book and however foolish the book may be no one must make fun of it or tell her how it goes on. It is still as it always was real to her.

GERTRUDE STEIN

Usually I read several books at a time—old books, new books, fiction, nonfiction, verse, anything—and when the bedside heap of a dozen volumes or so has dwindled to two or three, which generally happens by the end of one week, I accumulate another pile.

VLADIMIR NABOKOV

People say that life is the thing, but I prefer reading.

LOGAN PEARSALL SMITH

Let us have done with this vociferous, hypocritical humbug about real life being so much more important than books.

JOHN COWPER POWYS

I read constantly. If I don't have a good book, I'm beside myself.

GAIL GODWIN

I'm a voracious reader. You have to read to survive. People who read for pleasure are wasting their time. Reading isn't fun; it's indispensable.

WOODY ALLEN

By the age of three, . . . I was already an addicted reader. I still crave daily immersion in experience other than my own; (it needn't be more pleasant, exciting or illuminating—merely other) and I still fall into books as though into catalepsy.

BRIGID BROPHY

If you can read silently you can read aloud. It takes practice, sure, but it's like playing the guitar: You don't have to be Doc Watson, you can get and give pleasure just pickin'. And a second point: A lot of the stuff we were taught to read silently—Jane! You are moving your lips!—reads better out loud.

URSULA K. LEGUIN

Literature illuminates life only for those to whom books are a necessity. Books are unconvertible assets, to be passed on only to those who possess them already.

ANTHONY POWELL

Blessings be the inventor of the alphabet, pen and printing press! Life would be—to me in all events—a terrible thing without books.

L. M. MONTGOMERY

I'll spend the rest of my life reading, and because I'd rather read than do anything else, I don't look forward to years of hopeless, black despair. Most men who are in for life are filled with bitterness and hatred for the unkind fate that led them to such a horrible end.

WILLIE SUTTON

Befiehl' dem Herrn deine Wege
u. hoffe auf ihn er wirds wohl
machen.

What the writer may reasonably ask from the public is more curiosity, more readiness to come within his reach and see whether he can shock them into a new way of looking at life. He has a right to ask that they should approach a book with the definite expectation of being disturbed, and with the knowledge that the finest pleasure literature can offer is the revelation which follows upon this shock to fixed habits of thinking and feeling.

JOHN MIDDLETON MURRY

And, though reading may not at first blush seem like an act of creation, in a deep sense it is. Without the enthusiastic reader, who is really the author's counterpart and very often his most secret rival, a book would die.

HENRY MILLER

What I want is to possess my readers while they are reading my book—if I can, to possess them in ways that other writers don't. Then let them return, just as they are, to a world where everybody else is working to change, persuade, tempt, and control them. The best readers come to fiction to be free of all that noise, to have set loose in them the consciousness that's otherwise conditioned and hemmed in by all that *isn't* fiction.

PHILIP ROTH

Occasionally I come across a book which I feel has been written especially for me and for me only. Like a jealous lover, I don't want anybody else to hear of it. To have a million such readers, unaware of each other's existence, to be read with passion and never talked about, is the daydream, surely, of every author.

W. H. AUDEN

I think I write in order to discover on my shelf a new book which I would enjoy reading. . . . An author, unfortunately, can never experience the sensation of reading his own work as though it were a book he had never read.

THORNTON WILDER

The way [the writer] shapes a line, the way he fashions a scene, the way he is implicit or explicit, bears in mind the reader he might be himself, if he were not a writer, and the fiction he would like to read if he were not obliged to write it.

WRIGHT MORRIS

I am a bad reader. I think most writers are bad readers. We just cannot immerse ourselves in a book. Our own thoughts get in the way; we start thinking what we could do if we had the book to write ourselves.

ANTHONY BURGESS

I read . . . without any particular respect for his material; respect for material is what the author ought to feel, not the reader. On the other hand, the reader ought to have respect for the writing, for the author's skill, and ought to judge a work of literature, disregarding its subject matter, first of all for the excellence of its workmanship.

HERMANN HESSE

In Africa, when you pick up a book worth reading, out of the deadly consignments which good ships are being made to carry out all the way from Europe, you read it as an author would like his book to be read, praying to God that he may have it in him to go on as beautifully as he has begun. Your mind runs, transported, upon a fresh deep green track.

ISAK DINESEN

We readers can be . . . what the writer himself would want us to be: a public that reads a *lot*—that reads widely, joyfully, and naturally; a public . . . that reads with the calm and ease and independence that comes from liking things in themselves, for themselves.

RANDALL JARRELL

When one can read, can penetrate the enchanted realm of books, why write?

COLETTE

We have our responsibilities as readers and even our importance. The standards we raise and the judgments we pass steal in the air and become part of the atmosphere which writers breathe as they work. An influence is created which tells upon them even if it never finds its way into print.

VIRGINIA WOOLF

I thank whatever gods may be that at 73 my taste for reading is undiminished, and another blessing at that age is that you no longer read what you *ought* to read, but what you want to.

GEORGE LYTTLETON

What is it that happens to one in consequence of his ceasing to read? He suffers a hardening of the intellectual arteries. . . . We all know many persons whose intellectual clock stopped some time ago, and there are people whose minds apparently froze at about the time when they should have begun to ripen, and which are like blocks of ice with a fish inside.

ROBERT CORTES HOLLIDAY

The man who reads can become older in experience by three thousand years; if he does not become thereby a little wiser also, the fault must be his. An active mind can develop as constant a hunger for the ideas as the body has for its daily bread. It is not the unhappiest type of mind. And its happiest hunting-ground must be found in books.

F. L. LUCAS

I am called to listen to the sound of my own heart—
to write the story within myself that demands to be
told at that particular point in my life. And if I do
this faithfully, clothing that idea in the flesh of human
experience and setting it in a true place, the sound
from my heart will resound in the reader's heart.

KATHERINE PATERSON

If the author's heart is, in reality, protected by the
sturdy wall that is the breastbone, on the pages of the
book it has no such bulwark. Anyone can read the
story and—loving it—take it in in a kind of literary
eucharist; cannibalism to its detractors, and the ultimate sharing to those of us who believe.

JANE YOLEN

In the beginning the word was with God; all explana
tions, physical and moral, rested on the divine. And
now for storytellers, even though those patterns of ex-
planation are strictly human, the word has not lost a
superhuman power to connect young and old, writer
and reader; to connect us with each other and with
the causes and consequences of what we do.

JILL PATON WALSH

There is nothing in which dishonesty or pretentiousness punishes itself so severely as it does with reading. It is like practicing religion because other people think better of you for doing so. Instead of helping people to be wise and tolerant and generous, it makes them despise true feeling and beautiful thought.

ARTHUR CHRISTOPHER BENSON

The secret, I suppose, of finding the best balance between life and books—a difficult one—is to hit the point where reading ceases to increase the aliveness of one's life, and begins to lessen it. For life is lessened when books start to encroach on real experience.

F. L. LUCAS

What we all hope, in reaching for a book, is to meet a man after our own heart, to experience tragedies and delights which we ourselves lack the courage to invite, to dream dreams which will render life more hallucinating, perhaps also to discover a philosophy of life which will make us more adequate in meeting the trials and ordeals which beset us. To merely add to our store of knowledge or improve our culture—whatever that may mean—seems worthless to me. I would rather see a man moved to crime, if he cannot be otherwise moved, than to see him grow more and more bookish.

HENRY MILLER

Every day I write more and read less, but I think that happens to all writers. We start by reading a lot and, as time passes, the balance changes. Anyway, I've done all the reading I need to do. I only read new books that friends strongly recommend.

CAMILO JOSE CELA

I think a writer has a responsibility to comment on our culture, to read other writers.

JOYCE CAROL OATES

In winter we close the windows
and read Chekhov
nearly weeping for his world.
What luxury, to be so happy
that we can grieve
over imaginary lives.

LISEL MUELLER

CHILDREN'S READING

The influence of early books is profound. So much of the future lies on the shelves; early reading has more influence on the conduct than any religious teaching.

GRAHAM GREENE

A child's story reading if it is rich lays open a world that lasts a lifetime; an impoverished, banal story world dulls the spirit forever.

ANGUS WILSON

A child without an acquaintance of some kind with a classic of literature . . . suffers from that impoverishment for the rest of his life. No later intimacy is like that of the first.

LIZETTE WOODWORTH REESE

To get the best out of books . . . you must begin to love these perennial friends very early in life. There is a glamour which you never see if you begin to read with a serious intention late in life, when questions of technique and grammar and mere words begin to seem too important.

MAURICE FRANCIS EGAN

Every child, when he first draws letters on his slate and makes his first attempts to read, thereby takes the initial step into an artificial and highly complicated realm whose laws and rules of play are too much to learn and fully employ in any one lifetime.

HERMANN HESSE

Books are still one of the most important ways that children extend the range of their experience. In the privacy of their reading, children can test their beliefs and perceptions without having to defend them against disapproving peers or parents. The writer's art and the reader's imagination free children to re-think, reassess and refeel their own attitudes about themselves, about others and about the world in which they live.

MARK JONATHAN HARRIS

There was wont to lie in my mother's parlour *Spensers Works*; this I happened to fall upon, and was infinitely delighted with the stories of the knights, and giants, and monsters, and brave horses, which I found everywhere there. . . . I think I had read him all over before I was twelve years old, and was thus made a poet as irremediably as a child is made an eunuch.

ABRAHAM COWLEY

I found in [my mother's] dressing room some odd volumes of Shakespeare, nor can I easily forget the rapture with which I sat up in my shirt reading them by the light of the fire in her apartment, until the bustle of the family rising from the supper warned me it was time to creep back to my bed, where I was supposed to have been safely deposited since nine o'clock.

SIR WALTER SCOTT

The world I had found out in Cooke's edition of the 'British Novelists' was to me a dance through life, a perpetual gala day. The sixpenny numbers of this work regularly contrived to leave off just in the middle of a sentence, and in the nick of a story. With what eagerness I used to look forward to the next number, and open the prints! Ah! never again shall I feel the enthusiastic delight with which I gazed at the figures, and anticipated the story and adventures.

WILLIAM HAZLITT

And how I felt it beat
Under my pillow, in the morning's dark,
An hour before the sun would let me read!
My books!

ELIZABETH BARRETT BROWNING

Twice five years,
Or less I might have been, when first my mind
With conscious pleasure opened to the charm
Of words in tuneful order, found them sweet
For their own sakes, a passion, and a power;
And phrases pleased me chosen for delight,
For pomp, or love.

WILLIAM WORDSWORTH

I had just taken to reading. I had just discovered the art of leaving my body to sit impassive in a crumpled up attitude in a chair or sofa, while I wandered over the hills and far away in novel company and new scenes.... My world began to expand very rapidly, ... the reading habit had got me securely.

H. G. WELLS

It was with a shock of pleasure that I turned the pages of my first real book. It was like hearing a vast wind, then looking up and seeing, beyond the Glanrafon woods, a curtain of cloud sweep up and away in gigantic folds, revealing the world.

EMLYN WILLIAMS

When I began to read the nursery rhymes for myself, and, later, to read other verses and ballads, I knew that I had discovered the most important things, to me, that could be ever. There they were, seemingly lifeless, made only of black and white, but out of them, out of their own being, came love and terror and pity and pain and wonder and all the other vague abstractions that made our ephemeral lives dangerous, great and bearable.

DYLAN THOMAS

JACKSON

There was an abandonment in reading in those days which I would fain catch again.... Words were intoxicants. I tasted, smelled, touched them. They were unknown fruit, strange and delectable, fragrance floating across wide seas, moonlight on still water. They were as remote from my stupid, halting speech as I was from my immediate and material surroundings. I never said them aloud, but I dwelt with them "in faery lands forlorn."

MARY ELLEN CHASE

I read them all, sometimes with shivers of puzzlement and sometimes with delight, but always calling for more. I began to inhabit a world that was two-thirds letterpress and only one-third trees, fields, streets and people. I acquired round shoulders, spindly shanks, and a despondent view of humanity. I read everything that I could find in English, taking in some of it but boggling most of it.

H. L. MENCKEN

As a little girl my greatest joy was to lose myself in a book—at first it was books with big pictures and few words and gradually books with many words and few or no pictures.... Today, many years later and millions of words later, I still get a positively physical pleasure from a beautifully carved sentence or a powerfully expressed idea.

ARIANNA STASSINOPOULOS HUFFINGTON

I recall reading with such intensity that my mother forbade me to go to the 82nd Street library because I was so inflamed with fairy stories I couldn't sleep.
RICHARD STERN

I am sure I read every book of fairy tales in our branch library, with one complaint—all that long golden hair. Never mind—my short brown hair became long and golden as I read and when I grew up I would write a book about a brown-haired girl to even things up.
BEVERLY CLEARY

I loved [fairy stories] so, and my mother weighed down by grief had given up telling me them. At Nohant I found Mmes. d'Ardnoy's and Perrault's tales in old editions which became my chief joy for five or six years. . . . I've never read them since, but I could tell each tale straight through, and I don't think anything in all one's intellectual life can be compared to these delights of the imagination.
GEORGE SAND

A fairy tale . . . demands of the reader total surrender; so long as he is in its world, there must be for him no other. . . . The way, the only way, to read a fairy tale is to . . . throw yourself in. There is no other way.
W. H. AUDEN

One of the great hardships of my childhood ... was that I could never find a decent place to read. If I tried to read at home in the living room, I was constantly pestered by someone saying, 'For goodness sake, Emily, move where it's light. You're going to ruin your eyes and no two ways about it,' or 'You ought to be outdoors with the other youngsters getting roses in your cheeks.' Of course I knew how to reply to all these kill-joy injunctions; to the first I said, 'They're *my* eyes,' and to the second, 'Getting some brains in my head is more important that getting any so-called roses in my cheeks.'

JEAN STAFFORD (*A Reading Problem*)

"Why don't you go and do something?" my mother would say.

"I *am* doing something. I'm reading."

"It isn't healthy just lying there with your nose in a book," she would say, just as she said to my father. Thus harassed, I would find places to read where I couldn't be found—in the attic, in the woods, and at night under the bedclothes with a flashlight.

ROBERT MACNEIL

When I was prig and my standards were low
Uncritical, unautocratic
I used to exult in Jack London and Poe,
Which I read in bed, bathroom, and attic.
Alas, that's the truth of my terrible youth.
Such the books I thought were away above par.
Gee, I thought they were great, in my juvenile
    state. . . .
And I still am convinced that they are.
    STEPHEN VINCENT BENÉT
    (*Books et Veritas*)

It is usual to speak in a playfully apologetic tone
about one's adult enjoyment of what are called 'children's books.' I think the convention is a silly one. . . .
The only imaginative works we ought to grow out of
are those which it would have been better not to have
read at all.
    C. S. LEWIS

From the very beginning I read books with the pleasure of rewriting them inside of me. When I was in
middle school, I read for the first time Dickens'
Pickwick Papers. I remember that as one of the great
festivals of my life. It was a moment when, without
realizing it, I was already writing. I actually felt the
pleasure of writing the *Pickwick Papers*.
    ANDREI BITOV

The author's hope and prayer is to share with the reader some of the imaginative excitement that went into creation and—more than that—to contribute to a small extent to the child reader's expanding imaginative landscape.

PENELOPE LIVELY

Children forced to read by their parents know how reading can be utterly denatured. The effects can last a lifetime—a whole lifetime, in which a book is something forbidden, unapproachable, an object of fear.

MARGUERITE DURAS

If reading becomes a bore, mental death is on the way. Children taught to read by tedious mechanical means rapidly learn to skim over the dull text without bothering to delve into its implications—which in time will make them prey to propaganda and to assertions based on scanty evidence, or none.

JOAN AIKEN

It's such a wonderful feeling to watch a child discover that reading is a marvelous adventure rather than a chore. I know that many writers for children say they do not write specifically with a child audience in mind. . . . This isn't true for me. I am very aware of my audience. Sometimes I can almost see them out there reacting as I write. Sometimes I think, 'Oh, you're going to like this part.'

ZILPHA KEATLEY SNYDER

It had been startling and disappointing to me to find out that story books had been written by *people,* that books were not natural wonders, coming up of themselves like grass.

EUDORA WELTY

The kind of response I hope for when I write my novels for children: to give them a chance to recognize something of their own feelings—about themselves, their parents, their friends—and their own situation as a kind of subject race, always at the mercy of the adults who mostly run their lives for them.

NINA BAWDEN

I believe children, even the youngest, love good language, and that they see, feel, understand and communicate more not less, than grownups. Therefore I never write down to them, but try to evoke that new, brilliant awareness that is their world.

LUCY M. BOSTON

We believe in books. Somehow we want to make childhood better, and we believe that a book given at the right moment can work magic in a child's life.

ANN SCHLEE

Children have a lot more to worry about from the parents who raised them than from the books they read.

E. L. DOCTOROW

As a child I felt that books were holy objects, to be caressed, rapturously sniffed, and devotedly provided for. I gave my life to them—I still do. I continue to do what I did as a child: dream of books, make books, and collect books.

MAURICE SENDAK

So great is the physical part of childish experiences, that books are indeed to them realities. They have their characteristics, to be detested or adored, in their make, feel, and look. The smell of some bindings, the surface of some papers, the tints of some illustrations seem to affect children, especially adversely, even when the contents of the books should have been favored.

EDMUND BLUNDEN

I believe that any book, however trashy and ephemeral, is good for a child if he finds pleasure in reading it. Any book that helps him to form a habit of reading, that helps to make reading one of his deep and continuing needs, is good for him.

RICHARD MCKENNA

There are perhaps no days of our childhood we lived so fully as those we believe we left without having lived them, those we spent with a favorite book.

MARCEL PROUST

I think it is a pity that [the young] do not learn to read for pleasure. They may presently find that an acquaintance with the great works of art and thought is the only real insurance against the barbarism of the time.

EDMUND WILSON

The greatest fun in reading aloud lies in the adventure of the thing—the sense of taking a child on an exploration of a fascinating territory into which you alone have penetrated.

LEONARD WIBBERLEY

You the reader, aided by your sidekick, are free to do just about anything, changing tempos, cutting lines, adding new ones, departing from the text entirely. As the child's breath thickens and there's a yawn or two, you might wind down to the softest of codas, or end abruptly, leaving the story line hanging at just the right spot, till next time. In short, free improv: reading to kids is to ordinary reading what jazz is to a string quartet.

SEAN WILENTZ

THE LIBRARY

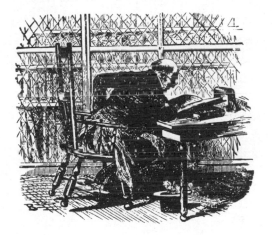

                              My library
Was dukedom large enough.
   WILLIAM SHAKESPEARE (*The Tempest*)

                                    That place that does
Contain my books, the best companions, is
To me a glorious court, where hourly I
Converse with the old sages and philosophers.
   JOHN FLETCHER

I no sooner come into the library, but I bolt the door
to me excluding lust, ambition, avarice, and all such
vices, whose nurse in idleness, the mother of ignorance and melancholy herself, and in the very lap of
eternity, amongst so many divine souls, I take my seat,
with so lofty a spirit and sweet content, that I pity all
our great ones, and rich men that know not this happiness.
   HEINSIUS

I am not ignorant . . . how barbarously and basely for
the most part our Tudor gentry esteem of libraries
and books, how they neglect and condemn so great a
treasure, so inestimable a benefit, as Aesop's cock did
the jewel he found in the dunghill; and all through
error, ignorance, and want of education.
   ROBERT BURTON

In a library we are surrounded by many hundreds of dear friends imprisoned by an enchanter in paper and leathern boxes.

RALPH WALDO EMERSON

Nothing is pleasanter than exploring a library.

WALTER SAVAGE LANDOR

A good library always makes me melancholy, where the best author is as much squeezed and as obscure as a porter at a coronation.

JONATHAN SWIFT

                                A cool of books
will sometimes lead the mind to libraries
of a hot afternoon, if books can be found
cool to the sense to lead the mind away.

For there is a wind or ghost of a wind
in all books echoing the life
there, a high wind that fills the tubes
of the ear until we think we hear a wind,
actual,

                                to lead the mind away.

WILLIAM CARLOS WILLAMS
(from *Paterson*)

People can lose their lives in libraries.
They ought to be warned.

SAUL BELLOW

When *I* want a book, it is as a tiger wants a sheep. I must have it with one spring, and, if I miss it, go away defeated and hungry. And my experience with public libraries is that the first volume of the book I inquire for is out, unless I happen to want the second, then *that* is out.

OLIVER WENDELL HOLMES

[I check out books at the library] because I've come to prefer reading a book that has already been read. I prefer the feel of the pages much as I prefer the feel of old leather to new leather. But more than this, I like how the library smells. Close your eyes and remember it: musty, dusty, gluey, eternal. I like to suck in a lungful of this book-sweet aroma, pick out a volume that has been kneaded by a hundred hands, then go read it under a tree.

LEE EISENBERG

When I . . . discovered libraries, it was like having Christmas every day.

JEAN FRITZ

The library smells, a combination of Lily of the Valley cologne, damp wells, library paste and wet wool snowsuits, were as distinctive as the smell of my childhood home.

JUDITH ST. GEORGE

There are quite a number of people in the reading-room; but one is not aware of them. They are inside the books. They move, sometimes, within the pages like sleepers turning over between two dreams. Ah, how good it is to be among people who are reading!

RAINER MARIA RILKE

In the reading room in the New York Public Library
All sorts of souls were bent over in silence reading the
  past,
Or the present, or maybe it was the future, persons
Devoted to silence and the flowering of the imag-
  ination.

RICHARD EBERHART
(from *Reading Room, The New York
Public Library*)

When I got [my] library card, that was when my life began.

RITA MAE BROWN

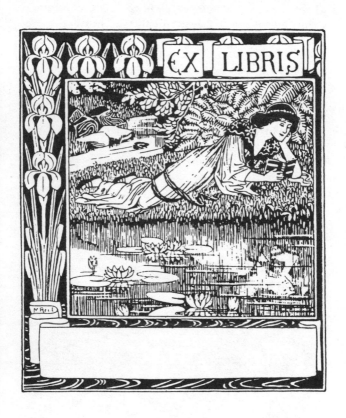

Whenever I need comfort, whenever I need some faint ray of hope, some desperate distraction from sadness, the library is where I find it. When life seems not worth living, ten minutes in the library proves otherwise.

You go in the door, not a single book to look for, who wants to read anyway? Here's a book on crocodiles—who can not read about crocodiles?

And then you are off, off in that other library world, floating in that happy sea where other books, ideas, reach out like fronds of seaweed to brush against your mind.

MIV SCHAAF

The library profession is . . . a profession that is informed, illuminated, radiated, by a fierce and beautiful love of books. A love so overwhelming that it engulfs community after community and makes the culture of our time distinctive, individual, creative and truly of the spirit.

FRANCES CLARKE SAYERS

The closest you will ever come in this life to an orderly universe is a good library.

ASHLEIGH BRILLIANT

The library, I believe, is the last of our public institutions to which you can go without credentials. . . . You don't even need the sticker on your windshield that you need to get into the public beach. All you need is the willingness to read.

HARRY GOLDEN

I have always imagined that Paradise will be a kind of library.

JORGE LUIS BORGES

BOOKSTORES

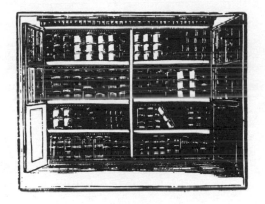

I yield to none in my love of bookstall urbanity. I have spent as many happy moments over the stalls (until the woman looked out), as any literary apprentice boy who ought to be moving onwards.

LEIGH HUNT

The secondhand stores are hospitable to the seeker of books. They are the only merchandising institutions which encourage the visitor to taste and often consume their wares before making a purchase, or even without making one.

WILLIAM F. MCDERMOTT

Some books are to be read in an hour, and returned to the shelf; others require a lifetime to savor their richness. Such books should be owned in personal copies, to travel with and to sleep beside—the most fruitful of all companions. Only your bookseller can consummate such a union of book and reader.

LAWRENCE CLARK POWELL

[B]ooksellers . . . are a race apart and one and all delightful company, as befits those in whom the ideal and the practical are so nicely blended. . . .

CYRIL CONNOLLY

To the secret race of collectors always ravenously de-
siring to get something for much less than its real
value, the windows of Riceyman Steps was ir-
resistible. . . . Collectors upon catching sight of the
shop exclaimed in their hearts: 'What a queer spot for
a bookshop! Bargains! . . . '

ARNOLD BENNETT (*Riceyman Steps*)

The bookstore is one of humanity's great engines . . .
one of the greatest instruments of civilization.

CHRISTOPHER MORLEY

To stand in a great bookshop crammed with books so
new that their pages almost stick together, and the gilt
on their backs is still fresh, has an excitement no less
delightful than the old excitement of the second-hand
bookstall.

VIRGINIA WOOLF

This bookstore on which bestowed all of my pocket
money, was a promised land, fragrant with the crisp
aroma of new books and uncut pages—an oasis for a
teenager with a newly acquired thirst for literature . . .
in a world that had little time for either.

SYLVIE DRAKE

BOOKS AS OBJECTS

Books are not made for furniture, but there is nothing else that so beautifully furnishes a house. The plainest row of books that cloth or paper ever covered is more significant of refinement than the most elaborately carved etagere or sideboard.

HENRY WARD BEECHER

To treat books as furniture is at any rate a better use for them than reading them; moreover it concerns the book as a material object. It deals with the outside of books which, ninety-nine times out of a hundred, is better than the inside.

HILAIRE BELLOC

At night, when the curtains are drawn and the fire flickers, and the lights are turned off, do [my books] come into their own, and attain a collective dignity. It is very pleasant to sit with them in the firelight for a couple of minutes, not reading, not even thinking, but aware that they, with their accumulated wisdom and charm, are waiting to be used, and that my library, in its tiny imperfect way, is a successor to the great private libraries of the past.

E. M. FORSTER

I rarely look at my books in that leisurely half-hour which precedes getting to work without fancying myself at the keyboard of an organ, the pipes of which are the gilded and many-colored rows of the shelves about me. One may have any kind of music he chooses; it is only a question of mood. There is no deep harmony, no haunting melody, ever heard by the spirit of man which one may not hear if he knows his book thoroughly

HAMILTON WRIGHT MABIE

Your house, being the place in which you read, can tell us the position books occupy in your life, if they are a defense you set up to keep the outside world at a distance, if they are a dream into which you sink as if into a drug, or bridges you cast toward the outside, toward the world that interests you so much that you want to multiply and extend its dimensions through books.

ITALO CALVINO

How I loved the authors of [my] books; how I loved them too, not only for the imaginative pleasures they afforded me, but for their making me love the very books themselves, and delight to be in contact with them.

LEIGH HUNT

The sight of the cover of a book one has previously read retains, woven into the letters of its title, the moonbeams of a far-off summer night.

MARCEL PROUST

Books, books, books in all their aspects, in form and spirit, their physical selves and what reading releases from their hieroglyphic pages, in their sight and smell, in their touch and feel to the questing hand, and in the intellectual music which they sing to thoughtful brain and loving heart, books are to me the best of all symbols, the realest of all reality.

LAWRENCE CLARK POWELL

There is no true love without some sensuality. One is not happy in books unless one loves to caress them. I recognize a true book-lover at the first glance by the manner in which he touches a book. The man who puts his hand on some precious, rare, lovable or at least, seemly volume, and who does not press it with a hand both gentle and firm, who does not voluptously pass a tender palm over its back, its sides, and its edges, that man never had the instinct that makes Groliers and Doubles.

ANATOLE FRANCE

There's so much more to a book than just reading. I've seen children play with books, fondle books, smell books, and that's every reason why books should be lovingly produced.

MAURICE SENDAK

I think *books* influenced me more than any title. I was entranced by the volume as an object, stiff covers between which were several hundred pages of magical symbols called print. I could flip them and cause a breeze against my cheek, thus demonstrating certain principles of physics. I could make a stack and see them a few feet away as a pyramid of print, a Pennine of pages. They appeared to me as stepping-stones to some state that I didn't yet know about.

ALAN SILLITOE

There was a time when I really did love books—loved the sight and smell and feel of them, I mean, at least if they were fifty or more years old. Nothing pleased me quite so much as to buy a job lot of them for a shilling at a country auction. There is a peculiar flavor about the battered unexpected books you pick up in that kind of collection.

GEORGE ORWELL

If I were rich I would have many books, and I would pamper myself with bindings bright to the eye and soft to the touch, paper generously opaque, and type such as men designed when printing was very young. I would dress my gods in leather and gold, and burn candles of worship before them at night, and string their names like beads on a rosary.

WILL DURANT

[Books] perfume and give weight to a room, which without books suffers from amnesia. A bookcase is as good as a view, as much of a panorama as the sight of a city or a river. There are dawns and sunsets in books—storms, fogs, zephyrs.

ANATOLE BROYARD

A precious—mouldering pleasure—'tis—
To meet an Antique Book—
In just the Dress his Century wore—
A privilege—I think—

EMILY DICKINSON

Demoyte's books were all behind glass, so that the room was full of reflections. Demoyte was a connoisseur of books. Spotless, gilded and calved, books to be held gently in the hand and admired, and which recalled to mind the fact that ... a book is a thing and not just a collection of thoughts.

IRIS MURDOCH (*The Sandcastle*)

[Douglas Jerrold] had an almost reverential fondness for books—books themselves—and said he could not bear to treat them, or see them treated, with disrespect. He told us it gave him pain to see them turned on their faces, stretched open, or dog's-eared, or carelessly flung down, or in any way misused.

GERALD & MARY COWDEN CLARKE

She was one of those who don't like the feel of prize books in their hands, and all of Wemyss's books might have been presented as prizes to deserving boys . . . She couldn't imagine idly turning their pages in some lazy position out on the grass. Besides, their pages wouldn't be idly turned; they would be, she was sure, obstinate with expensiveness, stiff with the leather and gold of their covers.

ELIZABETH (*Vera*)

You can't read a book without thinking about the origins of those little characters we call type. They were designed to express a thought, an idea; and placed next to each other, they might change the world—as they often have. The typeface chosen should reflect the book's content, contribute to the clarity of the ideas expressed, and be read with ease. Like notes in a musical score, those letters should cling to you, continue to grow in your mind, and develop understanding and sensitivity—a sense of the quality of life.

FRITZ EICHENBERG

[Books] also had a meaning for her as physical objects: she loved to walk down the street with a book under her arm. It had the same significance for her as an elegant cane for the dandy a century ago. It differentiated her from others.

MILAN KUNDERA (*The Unbearable Lightness of Being*)

Like the faces of human beings, [books] develop character as they age. Is there a more pleasant room in a house than a library, a jungle more filled with adventure than a secondhand bookstore?

ERIK CHRISTIAN HAUGAARD

If a book is worth reading, it is worth buying. No book is worth anything which is not worth *much;* nor is it serviceable until it has been read, and re-read, and loved, and loved again; and marked, so that you can refer to the passages you want in it, as a soldier can seize the weapon he needs in an armory; or a housewife bring the spice she needs from her store.

JOHN RUSKIN

[Your books] take on something of your personality, and your environment also—you know a second-hand book sometimes is so much more flesh and blood than a new one   and it is almost terrible to think that your ideas, yourself in your books, may be giving life to generations of readers after you are forgotten.

T. E. LAWRENCE

[O]ne cannot begin too soon to buy one's own books, if for no other reason ... than the freedom which they give to use their fly-leaves for your own private index of those matters in their pages which are particularly yours, whether for interest, or information, or for what not—those things which the index makers never by any possibility include.

JOHN LIVINGSTON LOWES

173

To compensate a little for the treachery and weakness of my memory, so extreme that it has happened to me more than once to pick up again ... books which I have read carefully a few years before. I have adopted the habit for some time now of adding at the end of each book the time I finished reading it and the judgment I have derived of it as a whole, so that this may represent to me at least the sense and general idea I had conceived of the author in reading it.

MICHEL DE MONTAIGNE

It seems to me as natural and necessary to keep notes, however brief of one's reading, as logs of voyages or photographs of one's travels. For memory, in most of us, is a liar with galloping consumption.

F. L. LUCAS

What a pity it is that all owners of books do not put their signatures on a fly-leaf! ... Our predecessors in proprietorship shared our tastes, and if they had taken the trouble to write their names, they might receive from us, and we from them, a slight telepathic impact of a friendly character.

ANDREW LANG

On the fly-leaves of these old prayer-books
  The childish writings fade,
Which show that once they were their books
  In the days when prayer was made
For other kings and princesses,
  William and Adelaide.
    JOHN MEADE FALKNER (from *Christmas Day*)

Most of us who read a lot are abysmally ignorant of books themselves, their fate and history; we cannot tell the difference between a roll and a codex, a chapbook and a plaquette, a colophon and an uncial.
    CYRIL CONNOLLY

COLLECTING

I am a book-collector, a proud avocationist in what Eric Quayle (wrongly) asserts to be the "least vicious" of hobbies (we are quite savage). We collectors are puzzled and often piqued unpleasantly by the common, absurd notion whereby we are only a pack of myopic, semi-crazed old pedants fretting over a book's colophon, dull dogs full of humorless zeal and no conversation, who suck our fingers free of pounce.

PAUL THEROUX

Book lovers are thought by unbookish people to be gentle and unworldly and perhaps a few of them are so. But there are those who will lie and scheme and steal to get books as wildly and unconscionably as the dope-taker in pursuit of his drug. They may not want the book to read immediately, or at all; they want them to possess, to range on their shelves, to have at command.

ROBERTSON DAVIES (*Tempest-Tost*)

A book collector is like a lighthouse keeper who offers sanctuary to buffeted and exhausted migrants as they home towards the friendly beam. Once behind glass they are safe from pollution . . . The envy, vanity and competitiveness of collectors are a minor phenomenon compared to the satisfaction with which they contemplate 'the precious life-blood of a master spirit' in its well-cared-for envelope.

CYRIL CONNOLLY

The really important thing in books is the words in them—words, the wine of life—not their bindings or their print, not their edition value or their bibliomaniac value, or their uncuttability.

E. M. FORSTER

Bibliomania and genuine love of literature are not the same thing. A man may have a passion for the accumulation of books who has no real enjoyment in the books themselves. I knew of a man who collected a large library, and was himself so ignorant that it was with difficulty he could read the title-page of any one of the thousands of books upon his shelves.

FREDERIC ROWLAND MARTIN

I am also very well pleased to hear that you have such a knowledge of, and taste for curious books and scarce and valuable tracts. This is a kind of knowledge which very well becomes a man of sound and solid learning, but which only exposes a man of slight and superficial reading; therefore, pray make the substance and matter of such books your first object, and their title-pages, indexes, letter, and binding, but your second.

EARL OF CHESTERFIELD

You will find then in the libraries of the most arrant idlers all that orators or historians have written—bookcases built up as high as the ceiling. Nowadays a library takes rank with a bathroom as a necessary ornament of a house. I could forgive such ideas, if they were due to extravagant desire for learning. As it is, these productions of men whose genius we revere, paid for at a high price, with their portraits ranged in line above them, are got together to adorn and beautify a wall.

LUCIUS ANNAEUS SENECA

As soon as I enter his house I am ready to faint on the staircase from a strong smell of morocco leather; in vain he shows me fine editions, gold leaves, and Etruscan bindings, naming them one after another as if he were showing a gallery of pictures! A gallery by the way he seldom traverses when alone, for he rarely reads, but me he offers to conduct through it! I thank him for his politeness, and, as little as himself, care to visit the tan-house which he calls his library.

BRUYÈRE

The non-reading of books [is the] characteristic of collectors. . . . Experts will bear me out when I say it is the oldest thing in the world. Suffice it to quote the answer which Anatole France gave to a philistine who admired his library and then finished with the standard question. 'And you have read all these books, Monsieur France?' 'Not one-tenth of them. I don't suppose you use your Sèvres china every day?'

WALTER BENJAMIN

There are two sorts of book collecting: of books fine and memorable in themselves, and of 'items' that are merely rare—and generally monstrously expensive. Devotees of the second sort of collecting I suspect of being just such exhibitionists as are the dreary people who are renowned for having the largest house on Myrtle Avenue or the costliest limousine in Omaha or the longest string of honorary degrees in the university. . . . But the collection of books that are distinguished in themselves, that are a delight to the hand as they are to the eye, that are masterful in paper, in binding, in the arrangement of the page, this is not so very different from the collection of superior paintings. . . .

SINCLAIR LEWIS

The truly dedicated bibliophile will never waste time in reading books, which should be spent in collecting them.

ANONYMOUS

THE FUTURE

Nowadays everything grows old in a few hours; reputation fades, a work passes away in a moment. Everybody writes, nobody reads seriously.

FRANÇOIS RENÉ DE CHATEAUBRIAND

Even if good literature entirely lost currency with the world, it would still be abundantly worthwhile to continue to enjoy it by oneself. But it never will lose currency with the world, in spite of momentary appearances; it never will lose supremacy. Currency and supremacy are insured to it, not indeed by the world's deliberate and conscious choice, but by something far deeper—by the instinct of self-preservation in humanity.

MATTHEW ARNOLD

We need not fear a future elimination of the book. On the contrary, the more that certain needs for entertainment and education are satisfied through other inventions, the more the book will win back in dignity and authority. For even the most childish intoxication with progress will soon be forced to recognize that writing and books have a function that is eternal. It will become evident that formulation in words and the handing on of these formulations through writing are not only important aids but actually the only means by which humanity can have a history and continuing consciousness of itself.

HERMANN HESSE

It is not the so-called bad books whose influence I deplore as much as the mediocre ones. The mediocre work, which is the daily fare for most of us, I regard as harmful because it is produced by automatons for automatons. And it is the automatons among us who are more of a hazard to society than the evil ones. If it is our fate to be destroyed by a bomb, it is the sleepwalker who is most apt to do the trick.

HENRY MILLER

It is very unlikely that the computer will displace the books, except in areas where we need information speedily—for police purposes or technological or scientific purposes. The book, with its intimacy, its forcibility, its accessibility, its freedom from outside energy sources, its ability to reach into tyrannic countries, and be hidden under mattresses, and be smuggled in the false bottoms of suitcases—all these are great advantages.

DANIEL J. BOORSTIN

I think it is good that books *still* exist, but they make me sleepy.

FRANK ZAPPA

I believe books will never disappear. It is impossible for it to happen. Of all mankind's diverse tools, undoubtedly the most astonishing are his books. . . . If books were to disappear, history would disappear. So would men.

JORGE LUIS BORGES

The smallest bookstore still contains more ideas of worth than have been presented in the entire history of television. . . . The book is the vessel that contains all the ideas that are good and important in our culture. As such it must be cherished, preserved, and protected.

ANDREW ROSS

[B]ooks will be here as long as humankind is. I know you can microfilm them and project the pages onto a screen. But there is no pleasure in holding microfilm in your hand.

ERIK CHRISTIAN HAUGAARD

The peoples of the West no longer share a literature and a system of ancient wisdom. All that they now have in common is science and information. Now, science is knowledge, not wisdom; deals with quantities, not with the qualities of which we are immediately aware. In so far as we are enjoying and suffering beings, its words seem to us mostly irrelevant and beside the point. Moreover, these words are arranged without art; therefore possess no magical power and are incapable of propping or moulding the mind of the reader.

ALDOUS HUXLEY

What about reading in the old, archaic, private, silent sense? This may become as specialized a skill and avocation as it was in the *scriptoria* and libraries of the monasteries during the so-called Dark Ages. . . . [T]he ability, above all, the wish to attend to a demanding text, to master the grammar, the arts of memory, the tactics of repose and concentration which great books demand of us—this may once more become the practice of an elite, of a mandarinate of silences.

GEORGE STEINER

Before I was aware of things in the world, the Penny Post had already begun to make a change adverse to reading, by consuming a vast amount of time in correspondence that was unnecessary, trivial, or irksome. Railways have altered people's habits by making them move about much more. . . . The motor-car is altogether unfavorable to reading . . . . The telephone is a deadly disadvantage; it minces time into fragments and frays the spirit. Wireless . . . is now being added as a distraction to divert people from reading. The cinematograph is another change in the same direction, and flying is becoming more and more common. All these things must make it more difficult for successive generations to acquire the habit of reading.

VISCOUNT GREY

There is the knowledge which reading can convey more swiftly and surely than whole armies of sages in the past, or all our multitudinous babblings out of boxes in the present. For one can read faster than anybody can talk. One can skip. One can reread what a first reading left obscure.

F. L. LUCAS

In our culture, TV—above all—dominates literacy. The authority of literature—if not the number of readers—has declined. But books need readers as well as publishers and writers. Literacy is a form of authority, it is not just a skill. There are desirable forms of literacy and empty forms. Writers, of course, are readers as well. When I taught creative writing I didn't produce writers, I was really teaching reading.

SUSAN SONTAG

The time will come when . . . there will be no more reading in the average home. Nor, perhaps, need one contemplate this prospect with apprehension, for by it literature will be liberated once more. That which the camera has achieved for painting, by freeing it from the necessity to record with photographic accuracy, [television] will accomplish for writing. The reading public will then be as loyal and enlightened as at the present moment are the lovers of poetry. . . . To this kind of public . . . the writer of the future will appeal. He may be conscious that only a few hundred thousand people, where today there is a possibility of millions, will read his books; but he will know that this public will follow with appreciative discernment every word from his pen.

OSBERT SITWELL

Reading is as private as thinking or dreaming, exactly; one imagines that it will be valued (and permitted) as long as private thinking and dreaming are valued and permitted.

JOHN BARTH

If only one person out of a hundred and fifty million should continue as a reader, he would be the one worth saving, the nucleus around which to found a university. . . . This Last Reader might very well stand in the same relation to the community as the queen bee to the colony of bees. . . . From his nuptial, or intellectual, flight would come the new race of men, linked perfectly with the long past by the unbroken chain of the intellect, to carry on the community.

E. B. WHITE

It's not books you need, it's some of the things that once were in books. The same things *could* be in the 'parlor families' today. The same infinite detail and awareness could be projected through the radios and televisors, but are not. No, no, it's not books at all you're looking for! Take it where you can find it, in the old phonograph records, old motion pictures, and in old friends; look for it in nature and look for it in yourself. Books were only one type of receptacle where we stored a lot of things we were afraid we might forget. There is nothing magical in them, at all. The magic is only in what books say, how they stitched the patches of the universe together into one garment for us.

RAY BRADBURY (*Fahrenheit 451*)

FOR THE BEST IN PAPERBACKS, LOOK FOR THE

In every corner of the world, on every subject under the sun, Penguin represents quality and variety—the very best in publishing today.

For complete information about books available from Penguin—including Pelicans, Puffins, Peregrines, and Penguin Classics—and how to order them, write to us at the appropriate address below. Please note that for copyright reasons the selection of books varies from country to country.

In the United Kingdom: For a complete list of books available from Penguin in the U.K., please write to *Dept E.P., Penguin Books Ltd, Harmondsworth, Middlesex, UB7 0DA*.

In the United States: For a complete list of books available from Penguin in the U.S., please write to *Dept BA, Penguin*, Box 120, Bergenfield, New Jersey 07621-0120.

In Canada: For a complete list of books available from Penguin in Canada, please write to *Penguin Books Ltd, 2801 John Street, Markham, Ontario L3R 1B4*.

In Australia: For a complete list of books available from Penguin in Australia, please write to the *Marketing Department, Penguin Books Ltd, P.O. Box 257, Ringwood, Victoria 3134*.

In New Zealand: For a complete list of books available from Penguin in New Zealand, please write to the *Marketing Department, Penguin Books (NZ) Ltd, Private Bag, Takapuna, Auckland 9*.

In India: For a complete list of books available from Penguin, please write to *Penguin Overseas Ltd, 706 Eros Apartments, 56 Nehru Place, New Delhi, 110019*.

In Holland: For a complete list of books available from Penguin in Holland, please write to *Penguin Books Nederland B.V., Postbus 195, NL-1380AD Weesp, Netherlands*.

In Germany: For a complete list of books available from Penguin, please write to *Penguin Books Ltd, Friedrichstrasse 10-12, D-6000 Frankfurt Main I, Federal Republic of Germany*.

In Spain: For a complete list of books available from Penguin in Spain, please write to *Longman, Penguin España, Calle San Nicolas 15, E-28013 Madrid, Spain*.

In Japan: For a complete list of books available from Penguin in Japan, please write to *Longman Penguin Japan Co Ltd, Yamaguchi Building, 2-12-9 Kanda Jimbocho, Chiyoda-Ku, Tokyo 101, Japan*.